"Being a delicious home baker doesn't have to be hard or require a bunch of expensive ingredients, and Jennifer is here to prove just that. Every recipe of Jennifer's that I have used has turned out to be easy, delicious and beautiful. *Quick-Shop-&-Prep 5 Ingredient Baking* is invaluable to all of us who enjoy baking for our families."

— STACEY LITTLE, author of *The Southern Bite Cookbook*

"*Quick-Shop-&-Prep 5 Ingredient Baking* brings together Jennifer's scrumptious recipes and fabulous flavors in a brilliant format that simplifies baking—something we can all use in our busy lives."

— CHRISTI JOHNSTONE, creator of the blog Love from the Oven and author of *Smart Cookie*

"Jennifer's recipes never fail to inspire me. They're simple, comforting and every bit as delicious as they look!"

— KRISTAN ROLAND, creator of the blog Confessions of a Cookbook Queen

"Jennifer's recipes always hit the mark. Her talent for combining ease of preparation, overall practicality with a touch of creativity has made her one of my go-to recipe sources."

— ANNA GINSBERG, winner of the 41st Pillsbury Bake-Off and blogger at Cookie Madness

"As a longtime fan of Jennifer's blog, I am thrilled that she finally has a cookbook! I love that by adding a few ingredients to what I already have in the pantry I can make amazing desserts. Baking from scratch has never been easier!"

— STEPHANIE PARKER, creator of the blog Plain Chicken

"For years Jennifer has been a go-to resource for making scrumptious baked goods that use ingredients you can find and are easy to make. Her approach to baking leads to delicious results with minimal effort."

— PEABODY JOHANSON, creator of the blog Culinary Concoctions by Peabody

"Jennifer's recipes are not only delicious, but they're easy to prepare. Quick and easy desserts are a sneaky way I get to spend extra time with my kids around the dinner table!"

— SHELLY JARONSKY, creator of the blog Cookies & Cups

QUICK-SHOP-&-PREP
5 INGREDIENT BAKING

COOKIES, CAKES, BARS & MORE THAT ARE EASIER THAN EVER TO MAKE

JENNIFER McHENRY
creator of the blog Bake or Break

PAGE STREET
PUBLISHING CO.

PAGE STREET
PUBLISHING CO.

First published in 2015 by
Page Street Publishing Co.
27 Congress Street, Suite 103
Salem, MA 01970
www.pagestreetpublishing.com

Distributed by Macmillan; sales in Canada by The Canadian Manda Group.

18 17 16 15   1 2 3 4 5

ISBN-13: 978-1-62414-154-6
ISBN-10: 1-62414-154-4

Library of Congress Control Number: 2015905657

Cover and book design by Page Street Publishing Co.
Photography by Jennifer and Quinn McHenry
Headshot by Kim Box Photography

Printed and bound in China

Page Street is proud to be a member of 1% for the Planet. Members donate one percent of their sales to one or more of the over 1,500 environmental and sustainability charities across the globe who participate in this program.

DEDICATION

For my mother, who understood the importance of cake for breakfast

CONTENTS

INTRODUCTION

I grew up surrounded by bakers. I don't mean professional bakers. No, these were great home bakers who took great joy and pride in serving homemade cakes, pies and more. In particular, I remember going to visit my grandmother or my great aunt and knowing with absolute certainty that there would be some kind of delicious sweet treat there just waiting to be served.

As I got older, I decided that I wanted to be like that. I wanted to have the home that always had homemade desserts just waiting for whoever might visit. That inspired me to embrace baking with that same joy and pride.

In 2006, I started writing about my baking adventures on my blog bakeorbreak.com. Over the years, I've worked my way from sharing other people's recipes to developing my own. What was once a side project for me has now become my full-time vocation and passion.

The more I baked, the more I began to realize that there is a short list of ingredients that are used over and over in baking recipes. I've kept a mental checklist of these items for a while now, always checking if they need to be replenished before shopping for groceries.

With those basic ingredients, you have the beginnings of a multitude of great from-scratch baked goods. Whether you're making a cake, brownies, muffins or some other baked treat, you'll need those essential ingredients to get started.

This collection of recipes is designed to allow you to maintain a simple baker's pantry and just add a few ingredients to make a fantastic variety of baked goods. We'll start by adding just two ingredients and work our way up to five additional ingredients. Along the way, we'll make simple treats like brownies and bars, comforting desserts like pie and decadent indulgences like cheesecake.

At the top of every recipe, you'll see a list of two to five extra ingredients you'll need to include in your shopping list to make the recipe. Simply add those to your stocked baker's pantry, and you're ready to roll!

THE BAKER'S PANTRY

Unbleached all-purpose flour

Unsalted butter

Eggs

Granulated sugar

Light brown sugar

Baking powder

Baking soda

Vanilla extract

Spices— cinnamon, nutmeg, ginger, black pepper, salt

THE BIG FOUR: FLOUR, BUTTER, EGGS, SUGAR

These four ingredients are the building blocks of traditional baking. Each brings something important to the formula for baking. These are the essentials that will show up in virtually every recipe in this book.

Flour's most important role is to help form gluten in baked goods, providing structure. It also plays a part in texture and flavor.

Every recipe in this book was developed with unbleached all-purpose flour. If you use bleached flour, keep in mind that the bleaching process often softens flour, leading to a difference in the texture of baked goods.

Tip: If you ask ten people to measure a cup of flour, you'll probably get ten surprisingly different results. That's why I highly recommend measuring flour by weight. If you don't have a scale, avoid scooping the measuring cup down into the flour to measure it. You'll likely compact the flour and end up with too much. And too much flour equals tough, chewy baked goods. Instead, fluff the flour and spoon it lightly into the measuring cup until it's overfilled. Then use a straight edge, such as the back of a knife, to scrape off the excess.

I include butter and eggs as baking pantry essentials despite their being refrigerated items. But honestly, you won't get very far with most baking without them. Butter makes baked goods tender and moist, and, best of all in my book, provides flavor. Eggs primarily help with structure but also contribute to flavor.

Tip: Different brands of salted butter contain varying amounts of salt. That's why I recommend baking exclusively with unsalted butter so that you can control the amount of salt in your recipe.

As you might guess, sugar is present in baking recipes to add sweetness. But it also helps make your baked goods soft and moist.

While granulated sugar is the most commonly used sugar in baking, I have a soft spot for brown sugar, so you're likely to find it in many of the recipes here. Brown sugar is made with a bit of molasses to add a little different flavor to your baking.

LEAVENING AGENTS: BAKING POWDER AND BAKING SODA

Most baked goods need help to rise. That's where leavening agents come into play. Baking powder and baking soda are the most commonly used leaveners and are essential to your baking pantry. Keep in mind that they are not interchangeable, because they react differently with the other ingredients in a recipe.

FLAVORS AND SPICES

The flavor of baked goods is influenced by all the ingredients in the recipe. Here, though, we're specifically talking about the ingredients that are added solely for flavor. Whether it's an extract or a spice, just a small measure of these can transform your baked goods into something delicious.

Over the years, *vanilla* has come to mean boring or bland. However, it is neither of those things. The little hint of vanilla you'll find in most baked goods adds another complexity to the flavor profile. While vanilla beans are often used in baking, vanilla extract is a perfect choice for stocking your pantry. For the best taste results, be sure to use pure vanilla extract instead of imitation vanilla.

I'm sure if we took a quick poll, we'd all have different spices that we consider essential because our taste preferences vary. The spices I've included as pantry staples—cinnamon, nutmeg, ginger, black pepper and salt—are the ones found in most of those spice starter sets you'll find in stores. If any are not usually included in those basic sets, I've called them out as extra ingredients.

LET'S BAKE SOMETHING!

Now that your baker's pantry is stocked, it's time to get baking! As with any recipe, be sure to read these all the way through before baking. That way you'll be well prepared and have everything you need.

Of course, our shopping and eating habits are all different, so you may have some of these additional items on hand. If you're a cereal eater, for instance, then you probably have milk in your refrigerator at all times. Also, once you acquire some of the other ingredients, many of them (such as oats or nuts) will have a long-enough shelf life that you'll have them on hand to use in other recipes.

Some ingredients are listed as optional. While these are not necessary for the recipe, they do add a little something extra in terms of flavor or appearance. So, consider using them if you already have them in your pantry or if you are looking to expand your pantry.

These recipes may be short on ingredients, but they are big on flavors and results. Each recipe is designed to be easy to make but without shortcuts. As you try these recipes, you can take pride in having baked something from scratch that can be shared with love.

+2 INGREDIENTS

While I generally tend to focus on simple recipes, the ones in this chapter are made even simpler by adding just two ingredients to your baking pantry staples. These recipes run the range from cookies to cakes to pies and even to cheesecake!

Some of my favorite flavor duos also shine here. My favorite sandwich combo gets the cookie treatment in Peanut Butter and Jelly Cookies (page 15). Ginger and lemon are a zesty pair in Lemon Ginger Scones (page 44). Cherry Yogurt Cake (page 20) showcases the classic combination of cherry and vanilla.

You'll quickly see how just a couple of ingredients can help you bake something extra special!

PEANUT BUTTER AND JELLY COOKIES

I've consumed more than my share of peanut butter and jelly sandwiches. There's just something irresistible about the combination of salty peanut butter and sweet jelly! I don't limit my enjoyment of PB&J to just sandwiches, though. It's a great pairing for dessert, too. These soft peanut butter cookies are wrapped around a bit of fruit filling for a sweet treat that's every bit as addicting as you'd think. I tend to prefer strawberry with my peanut butter, but feel free to use your favorite flavor to make these delicious cookies.

MAKES 18 COOKIES

1½ cups (180 g) unbleached all-purpose flour

½ tsp baking soda

½ tsp salt

½ cup (113 g) unsalted butter, softened

1 cup (255 g) creamy **peanut butter**

1 cup (200 g) firmly packed light brown sugar

1 large egg

1 tsp (5 ml) vanilla extract

3 tbsp (45 ml) **strawberry preserves**

Preheat the oven to 350°F (180°C). Line baking sheets with parchment paper or silicone liners.

Whisk together the flour, baking soda and salt. Set aside.

Using an electric mixer on medium speed, beat the butter, peanut butter and brown sugar until light and fluffy. Add the egg and vanilla, and mix well.

Reduce the mixer speed to low. Gradually add the flour mixture, mixing just until combined.

Using about 2 tablespoons (30 g) of dough at a time, roll the dough into balls. Flatten each ball into a disk. Place about ½ teaspoon of preserves in the center of the disk. Fold the edges of the disk around the preserves. Roll into a ball.

Place the cookies on the prepared baking sheets, leaving about 2 inches (5 cm) between cookies. Bake for 14 to 16 minutes, or until the cookies are lightly browned. Allow to cool on the pans for 5 minutes. Then transfer the cookies to a wire rack to cool completely.

APPLE CRUMB BARS

There's something so inherently comforting about apple desserts. Maybe it's how they make you think of crisp fall days, or maybe it's the pairing of sweet, tart apples with delicious spices, such as cinnamon. These tasty bars combine the best parts of apple pie and apple crumble into one dessert.

MAKES 24 BARS

FOR THE CRUST AND CRUMB TOPPING

2½ cups (300 g) unbleached all-purpose flour

1½ cups (120 g) **old-fashioned rolled oats**

½ cup (100 g) firmly packed light brown sugar

¼ tsp ground cinnamon

¼ tsp salt

1 cup (226 g) unsalted butter, cold, cut into small cubes

FOR THE FILLING

4 medium **apples**, cored and chopped or sliced

½ cup (100 g) firmly packed light brown sugar

2 tbsp (28 g) unsalted butter

2 tsp (5 g) ground cinnamon

Preheat the oven to 350°F (180°C). Grease a 9 x 13 x 2-inch (23 x 33 x 5-cm) baking pan.

TO MAKE THE CRUST AND CRUMB TOPPING

Combine the flour, oats, brown sugar, cinnamon and salt in a bowl. Add the butter, and mix with a pastry blender or a fork until the mixture is combined and crumbly. The mixture should hold together when pinched.

Reserve about a cup (120 g) of the crust mixture for the topping. Press the remaining crust mixture firmly and evenly into the prepared pan. Bake for 20 minutes. Set aside.

TO MAKE THE FILLING

Place the apples, brown sugar, butter and cinnamon in a skillet and stir to combine. Cook over medium heat, stirring occasionally, for 10 minutes, or until the mixture is soft and bubbly.

Spread the filling evenly over the partially baked crust. Sprinkle the reserved crust mixture over the top of the filling.

Bake for 45 to 50 minutes, or until the edges and topping are golden brown. Allow to cool in the pan for 15 minutes before cutting into bars.

TIP: Not all apples are good choices for baking. Available apple varieties will vary by region, so look for apples that aren't too sweet and are crisp enough that they won't fall apart during baking. Some of my favorites are Pink Lady, Fuji and Jonagold.

WHITE CHOCOLATE COCONUT COOKIES

I love all things coconut, and white chocolate is one of my favorite flavors to pair with it. The lovely sweetness of each complements the other perfectly. I prefer to use unsweetened shredded coconut for these cookies for a couple of reasons. First of all, the shredded pieces work better as a coating for the cookies. And second, unsweetened coconut lets the natural flavor of the coconut really shine.

MAKES 40 COOKIES

2 cups (240 g) unbleached all-purpose flour

1 tsp (5 g) baking powder

½ tsp salt

1 cup (226 g) unsalted butter, softened

¾ cup (150 g) granulated sugar

1 large egg

1 tsp (5 ml) vanilla extract

4 oz (113 g) **white chocolate chips**

½ cup (40 g) **unsweetened shredded coconut**

Whisk together the flour, baking powder and salt. Set aside.

Using an electric mixer on medium speed, beat the butter and sugar until light and fluffy. Mix in the egg and vanilla.

Reduce the mixer speed to low. Gradually add the flour mixture, mixing just until combined. Stir in the white chocolate. Refrigerate the dough for 30 minutes.

Preheat the oven to 350°F (180°C). Line baking sheets with parchment paper or silicone liners.

Using a tablespoonful (15 g) of dough at a time, roll the dough into balls. Place the coconut in a shallow bowl. Roll each dough ball in the coconut, coating thoroughly.

Place the cookies on the prepared pans, leaving about 2 inches (5 cm) between cookies. Bake for 12 to 15 minutes, or until the edges of the cookies are lightly browned. Allow to cool on the pans for 10 minutes. Then transfer the cookies to a wire rack to cool completely.

CHERRY YOGURT CAKE

At first glance, pairing cherries with vanilla may not seem all that exciting, but I assure you that it is actually quite worthy of excitement. The two really bring out the best in each other.

When cherry season hits, this is the kind of dessert I want to make. It's simple, soft and full of fresh flavor. I like to use whole cherries in this cake so that I get big bites throughout the cake. If you prefer smaller bites, cut the cherries into halves or quarters.

MAKES 16 SERVINGS

1¼ cups (150 g) unbleached all-purpose flour

1 tsp (5 g) baking powder

¼ tsp baking soda

¼ tsp salt

6 tbsp (84 g) unsalted butter, softened

¾ cup (150 g) granulated sugar

1 large egg

1 tsp (5 ml) vanilla extract

½ cup (114 g) **vanilla yogurt**

1 cup (175 g) **cherries**, pitted

Confectioners' sugar (optional)

Preheat the oven to 350°F (180°C). Grease an 8 x 8 x 2-inch (20 x 20 x 5-cm) baking pan.

Whisk together the flour, baking powder, baking soda and salt. Set aside.

Using an electric mixer on medium speed, beat the butter and sugar until light and fluffy. Add the egg and vanilla, and mix well. Mix in the yogurt.

Reduce the mixer speed to low. Gradually add the flour mixture, mixing just until combined.

Spread the batter evenly in the prepared pan. Scatter the cherries over the top of the batter.

Bake for 35 to 40 minutes, or until a pick inserted into the center comes out clean. Allow the cake to cool completely in the pan before serving. If desired, sprinkle with confectioners' sugar before serving.

GLAZED CINNAMON SHORTBREAD

Shortbread is one of the baking world's simplest treats. These eggless cookies
are quick to make and only require one mixing bowl. Cinnamon adds big flavor to these little cookies.
Dipping them in a sweet glaze is the perfect finish!

MAKES 24 COOKIES

FOR THE SHORTBREAD

¾ cup (170 g) unsalted butter, softened

½ cup (100 g) granulated sugar

½ tsp vanilla extract

1½ cups (180 g) unbleached all-purpose flour

1½ tsp (4 g) ground cinnamon

¼ tsp salt

2 to 4 tsp (10 to 20 ml) water

FOR THE CONFECTIONERS' SUGAR GLAZE

1 cup (110 g) **confectioners' sugar**, sifted

1 to 2 tbsp (15 to 30 ml) **milk**

TO MAKE THE SHORTBREAD

Using an electric mixer on medium speed, beat the butter, sugar and vanilla until light and fluffy.

Reduce the mixer speed to low. Add the flour, cinnamon and salt, and mix just until combined. Mix in 2 teaspoons (10 ml) of the water. If necessary, add more water, a small amount at a time, so that the mixture forms a dough.

Gather the dough into a ball and flatten into a disk about ¾-inch (2-cm) thick. Cover the dough in plastic wrap and refrigerate for 1 hour.

Preheat the oven to 325°F (160°C). Line baking sheets with parchment paper or silicone liners.

Place the dough on a lightly floured surface. Roll the dough into a circle ¼-inch (0.6-cm) thick. Use a 2-inch (5-cm) round cookie cutter to cut the dough into rounds.

Transfer the cookies to the prepared pans. Bake for 18 to 22 minutes, or until lightly browned. Allow to cool on the pans for 10 minutes. Then transfer the cookies to a wire rack to cool completely.

TO MAKE THE CONFECTIONERS' SUGAR GLAZE

Stir together the confectioners' sugar and 1 tablespoon (15 ml) of milk. If necessary, add the remaining milk, a small amount at a time, until the glaze is the desired consistency.

Dip half of each cookie into the glaze. Place the cookies on a wire rack to allow the glaze to set.

CHOCOLATE CHIP QUICK BREAD

Quick breads don't have to be all nuts and fruits. This one gets its flavor from plenty of chocolate chips!
This bread is on the denser end of the quick bread spectrum. It's just the thing to have
in your kitchen for snack time or for a coffee companion.

MAKES 8 TO 10 SERVINGS

FOR THE TOPPING

⅓ cup (40 g) unbleached all-purpose flour

⅓ cup (67 g) firmly packed light brown sugar

2 tbsp (21 g) **mini semisweet chocolate chips**

2 tbsp (28 g) unsalted butter, cold, cut into small cubes

FOR THE BREAD

2 cups (240 g) unbleached all-purpose flour

1 cup (200 g) granulated sugar

1 tsp (5 g) baking powder

½ tsp baking soda

¼ tsp salt

½ cup (113 g) unsalted butter, melted and slightly cooled

½ cup (114 g) **sour cream**

2 large eggs

1 tsp (5 ml) vanilla extract

1 cup (170 g) **mini semisweet chocolate chips**

TO MAKE THE TOPPING

Combine the flour, brown sugar and chocolate chips. Add the butter and mix with a pastry blender or a fork until the mixture forms crumbs. Set aside while you make the bread.

TO MAKE THE BREAD

Preheat the oven to 375°F (190°C). Grease a standard 9 x 5 x 3-inch (23 x 13 x 8-cm) loaf pan.

Whisk together the flour, granulated sugar, baking powder, baking soda and salt in a large mixing bowl.

In a separate bowl, stir together the butter, sour cream, eggs and vanilla.

Make a well in the center of the dry ingredients. Add the butter mixture and stir until a few streaks of flour remain. Stir in the chocolate chips just until the mixture is combined.

Transfer the batter to the prepared pan and spread evenly. Sprinkle the topping over the batter. Bake for 40 to 45 minutes, or until a pick inserted into the center comes out clean. Allow to cool in the pan for 15 minutes before serving.

BROWN BUTTER CHOCOLATE CHIP PIE

My dear friend Tonya and I have long shared a love of baking and cooking and have been swapping recipes for years. One day she sent me a recipe for a chocolate chip pie from her grandmother's recipe box. I was so intrigued by it that I kept going back to it over and over again. My version ups the flavor ante with browned butter. If you've never baked with browned butter before, you are in for a treat and perhaps a new addiction. It adds such a wonderful, nutty, rich flavor that makes this pie fantastic!

MAKES 8 TO 10 SERVINGS

FOR THE BASIC BUTTER PIE CRUST

1¼ cups (150 g) unbleached all-purpose flour

1 tsp (4 g) granulated sugar

½ tsp salt

½ cup (113 g) unsalted butter, cold, cut into small cubes

3 to 4 tbsp (45 to 60 ml) cold water

FOR THE FILLING

10 tbsp (141 g) unsalted butter, sliced

½ cup (100 g) granulated sugar

½ cup (100 g) firmly packed light brown sugar

2 large eggs

1 tsp (5 ml) vanilla extract

½ cup (60 g) unbleached all-purpose flour

½ tsp salt

1 cup (170 g) **semisweet chocolate chips**

1 cup (120 g) **pecans**, chopped

TO MAKE THE BASIC BUTTER PIE CRUST

Combine the flour, granulated sugar and salt in a large bowl. Add the butter and mix with a pastry blender or a fork until the largest pieces of butter are about the size of large peas. Add the water, about a tablespoon (15 ml) at a time, and mix until a dough forms.

Shape the dough into a ball, place on a sheet of plastic wrap, and flatten slightly into a disk about 1-inch (2.5-cm) thick. Wrap the dough tightly in plastic wrap and refrigerate for at least 2 hours.

Place the chilled dough on a lightly floured surface. Roll the dough into a circle ⅛ inch (0.3 cm) thick. Transfer the dough to a 9-inch (23-cm) round pie pan. Trim and crimp the edges as desired. Place the pie pan in the refrigerator while you prepare the filling.

TO MAKE THE FILLING

Preheat the oven to 350°F (180°C).

Place the butter in a medium, heavy saucepan. Cook over medium-low heat until the butter melts and begins to foam, about 3 minutes. Continue to cook, whisking occasionally, just until brown specks begin to form at the bottom of the pan and the butter has a nutty aroma. This should take only 2 to 3 minutes. Remove the pan from the heat and whisk lightly for about 30 seconds. Transfer the butter to a large mixing bowl and allow it to cool slightly. If desired, strain the butter to remove some of the browned bits.

Add the granulated sugar, brown sugar, eggs and vanilla to the cooled butter. Stir until thoroughly combined. Add the flour and salt, and mix just until combined. Stir in the chocolate chips and pecans.

Transfer the filling to the chilled pie crust, and spread the mixture evenly. Bake for 45 to 50 minutes, or until the crust is golden brown and the center of the pie is set. Allow to cool for 10 minutes before serving.

PEANUTTY BROWNIES

With the popularity of nuts like pecans and almonds, those poor peanuts tend to get overlooked. Sure, they aren't really nuts, but they do provide a nutty taste. These rich, cakelike brownies sit atop a simple shortbread crust made with honey-roasted peanuts. They lend a sweet, salty, nutty flavor and a nice crunch, making these brownies pretty much irresistible.

MAKES 16 BROWNIES

FOR THE CRUST

1 cup (120 g) unbleached all-purpose flour

¼ cup (50 g) firmly packed light brown sugar

½ cup (113 g) unsalted butter, cold, cut into small cubes

½ cup (60 g) **honey-roasted peanuts**, chopped

FOR THE BROWNIES

¾ cup (90 g) unbleached all-purpose flour

½ cup (40 g) **unsweetened cocoa powder**

½ tsp salt

10 tbsp (141 g) unsalted butter, melted and slightly cooled

1 cup (200 g) firmly packed light brown sugar

2 large eggs

1 tsp (5 ml) vanilla extract

TO MAKE THE CRUST

Preheat the oven to 350°F (180°C). Grease an 8 x 8 x 2-inch (20 x 20 x 5-cm) baking pan.

Combine the flour and brown sugar in a mixing bowl. Add the butter and mix with a pastry blender or a fork until combined. The dough will be crumbly, but it should hold together when pinched. Mix in the peanuts.

Press the dough evenly and firmly into the bottom of the prepared pan. Bake for 12 minutes. Set aside to cool slightly.

TO MAKE THE BROWNIES

Whisk together the flour, cocoa powder and salt. Set aside.

Stir together the melted butter, brown sugar, eggs and vanilla until thoroughly combined. Add the flour mixture and mix just until combined. Spread the batter evenly over the partially baked crust.

Bake for 35 to 40 minutes, or until a pick inserted into the center comes out with moist crumbs. Allow to cool in the pan for 10 mintues before cutting into bars.

BROWN BUTTER CINNAMON CRINKLE COOKIES

Crinkle cookies have long been one of the prettiest cookies in the baking world. Coating the cookies in confectioners' sugar really makes the cracks in the tops of the cookies stand out. As much as I love the aesthetics of these cookies, the flavor is what I really adore. Brown butter gives them a nutty flavor that combines perfectly with cinnamon and pecans. They are, in a word, outstanding!

MAKES 36 COOKIES

10 tbsp (141 g) unsalted butter, sliced

2½ cups (300 g) unbleached all-purpose flour

1 tsp (5 g) baking powder

1 tsp (2.5 g) ground cinnamon

½ tsp salt

1 cup (200 g) granulated sugar

¼ cup (50 g) firmly packed light brown sugar

2 large eggs

1 tsp (5 ml) vanilla extract

½ cup (60 g) **pecans**, chopped

¼ cup (28 g) **confectioners' sugar**

Place the butter in a medium, heavy saucepan. Cook over medium-low heat until the butter melts and begins to foam, about 3 minutes. Continue to cook, whisking occasionally, just until brown specks begin to form at the bottom of the pan and the butter has a nutty aroma. This should take only 2 to 3 minutes. Remove the pan from the heat and whisk lightly for about 30 seconds. Transfer the butter to a large mixing bowl and allow it to cool slightly. If desired, strain the butter to remove some of the browned bits.

Whisk together the flour, baking powder, cinnamon and salt. Set aside.

Add the granulated sugar and brown sugar to the cooled butter. Use an electric mixer on medium speed to mix thoroughly. Add the eggs, one at a time, mixing just until combined. Mix in the vanilla.

Reduce the mixer speed to low. Gradually add the flour mixture, mixing just until combined. Stir in the pecans. Cover the mixing bowl with plastic wrap, and refrigerate the dough for 1 hour.

Preheat the oven to 350°F (180°C). Line baking sheets with parchment paper or silicone liners.

Place the confectioners' sugar in a shallow bowl. Divide the dough into 1-tablespoon (15-g) portions. Roll each portion in the confectioners' sugar, coating thoroughly. Roll the dough into balls and place on the prepared pans, leaving about 2 inches (5 cm) between the cookies.

Bake for 18 to 22 minutes, or until the cookies are lightly browned and set. Allow to cool on the pans for 10 minutes. Then transfer the cookies to a wire rack to cool completely.

TIP: Don't be shy about coating these cookies in confectioners' sugar. Some of the sugar will be absorbed into the cookies as they bake, so a thick coating is essential to get the classic look of crinkle cookies.

POMEGRANATE POUND CAKE

Pomegranate juice is a frequent resident of my refrigerator. It's one of my favorite additions to smoothies and cocktails. One day as I moved a bottle of it aside to get to something or other, I wondered why I'd never baked with it. The juice is sweet with a bit of tartness. In this simple pound cake, the juice adds a subtle hint of that fantastic flavor for a delicious twist on a classic cake.

MAKES 8 TO 10 SERVINGS

2 cups (240 g) unbleached all-purpose flour

1 tsp (5 g) baking powder

¼ tsp salt

½ cup (113 g) unsalted butter, softened

1½ cups (300 g) granulated sugar

3 large eggs

3 tbsp (45 ml) **pomegranate juice**

½ tsp vanilla extract

¼ cup (60 ml) **milk**

Preheat the oven to 325°F (160°C). Grease a standard 9 x 5 x 3-inch (23 x 13 x 8-cm) loaf pan.

Whisk together the flour, baking powder and salt. Set aside.

Using an electric mixer on medium speed, beat the butter and sugar until light and fluffy. Add the eggs, one at a time, mixing well after each addition. Mix in the pomegranate juice and vanilla.

Reduce the mixer speed to low. Add about a third of the flour mixture, and mix just until there are a few streaks of flour remaining. Add about half of the milk, and mix until combined. Alternate mixing in two more portions of the flour mixture with the remaining portion of milk. Mix just until combined.

Transfer the batter to the prepared pan. Bake for 55 to 60 minutes, or until a pick inserted into the center comes out clean. Allow to cool in the pan for 10 minutes. Then invert the cake onto a wire rack to cool completely.

LEMON CHEESECAKE COOKIES

Lemons and cheesecake have been great pals for a long time. That hint of lemon tartness wonderfully complements the sweet, tangy flavor of cheesecake. Transform that tasty combination into handheld form with these cookies.

MAKES 48 COOKIES

2½ cups (300 g) unbleached all-purpose flour

1 tsp (5 g) baking powder

¼ tsp salt

Zest of 1 medium **lemon**

½ cup (113 g) unsalted butter, softened

8 oz (227 g) **cream cheese**, softened

2 cups (400 g) granulated sugar

2 large eggs

Juice of 1 medium **lemon**

Preheat the oven to 350°F (180°C). Line baking sheets with parchment paper or silicone liners.

Whisk together the flour, baking powder, salt and lemon zest. Set aside.

Using an electric mixer on medium speed, beat the butter, cream cheese and sugar until light and fluffy. Add the eggs, one at a time, mixing well after each addition. Mix in the lemon juice.

Reduce the mixer speed to low. Gradually add the flour mixture, mixing just until combined. The dough will be sticky.

Drop the dough by tablespoonfuls (15 g) onto the prepared pans. Bake for 12 to 16 minutes, or until the edges are lightly browned. These cookies do not brown much, so be careful not to overbake. Allow to cool on the pans for 10 minutes. Then transfer the cookies to a wire rack to cool completely.

CREAM CHEESE-FILLED CHOCOLATE CHIP BLONDIES

Blondies often don't get the same kind of attention that their brownie counterparts garner. Why that's the case is a bit of a mystery to me. I find all that brown sugar flavor hard to resist! These chocolate chip blondies have a ribbon of sweetened cream cheese running through them, making them even more delicious.

MAKES 16 BLONDIES

FOR THE BLONDIES

2 cups (240 g) unbleached all-purpose flour

½ tsp baking powder

½ tsp salt

¾ cup (170 g) unsalted butter, melted and slightly cooled

1 cup (200 g) firmly packed light brown sugar

2 large eggs

1½ tsp (7.5 ml) vanilla extract

¾ cup (128 g) **mini semisweet chocolate chips**

FOR THE FILLING

6 oz (170 g) **cream cheese**, softened

⅓ cup (67 g) granulated sugar

TO MAKE THE BLONDIES

Preheat the oven to 350°F (180°C). Grease an 8 x 8 x 2-inch (20 x 20 x 5-cm) baking pan.

Whisk together the flour, baking powder and salt. Set aside.

Using an electric mixer on medium speed, beat the butter and brown sugar until light and fluffy. Add the eggs, one at a time, mixing well after each addition. Mix in the vanilla.

Reduce the mixer speed to low. Gradually add the flour mixture, mixing just until combined. Stir in the chocolate chips.

Spread half of the mixture into the prepared pan.

TO MAKE THE FILLING

Beat the cream cheese and granulated sugar until smooth. Spread the mixture evenly over the blondies in the pan.

Carefully spread the remaining blondie mixture over the top of the cream cheese mixture.

Bake for 25 to 30 minutes, or until the blondies are lightly browned and set. Allow to cool in the pan for 15 minutes before cutting and serving.

TOFFEE PEAR CROSTATA

Crostatas are great to make if you're new to making pies or if you're looking to take a bit of a baking shortcut. You still get to enjoy the incomparable goodness of homemade pie crust, but you can bypass the pan in favor of a more rustic look. The toffee crumb topping is a wonderful complement to the sweet, cinnamon-y pears in the filling. Plus, I love that little bit of crunch the toffee provides.

MAKES 8 TO 10 SERVINGS

FOR THE BASIC BUTTER PIE CRUST

1¼ cups (150 g) unbleached all-purpose flour

1 tsp (4 g) granulated sugar

½ tsp salt

½ cup (113 g) unsalted butter, cold, cut into small cubes

3 to 4 tbsp (45 to 60 ml) cold water

FOR THE FILLING

4 medium **pears**, cored and sliced

3 tbsp (38 g) granulated sugar

1 tsp (2.5 g) ground cinnamon

FOR THE TOPPING

¼ cup (50 g) firmly packed light brown sugar

¼ cup (30 g) unbleached all-purpose flour

¼ cup (40 g) **toffee bits**

Pinch of salt

3 tbsp (42 g) unsalted butter, softened, cut into small cubes

1 large egg

1 tbsp (15 ml) water

Sanding sugar (optional) (see page 44)

TO MAKE THE BASIC BUTTER PIE CRUST

Combine the flour, granulated sugar and salt in a large bowl. Add the butter and mix with a pastry blender or a fork until the largest pieces of butter are about the size of large peas. Add the water, about a tablespoon (15 ml) at a time, and mix until a dough forms.

Shape the dough into a ball, place on a sheet of plastic wrap, and flatten slightly into a disk about 1-inch (2.5-cm) thick. Wrap the dough tightly in plastic wrap and refrigerate for at least 2 hours.

Preheat the oven to 400°F (200°C). Line a baking sheet with parchment paper.

Place the chilled pie dough on a lightly floured surface. Roll the dough into a circle ⅛-inch (0.3-cm) thick. Carefully transfer the crust to the prepared pan. Place the pan in the refrigerator while you prepare the filling.

TO MAKE THE FILLING

Combine the pears, granulated sugar and cinnamon. Spread the mixture evenly on the crust, leaving about a 1½ inch (4 cm) border. Fold the edges of the crust up and over the filling, leaving the center open and pressing the edges together to help prevent spills.

TO MAKE THE TOPPING

Combine the brown sugar, flour, toffee bits and salt. Add the butter and mix with a fork or your hands until the mixture forms crumbs. Sprinkle over the filling.

In a small bowl, lightly beat the egg and water to make an egg wash. Brush the top of the crust with the egg wash. You won't use all of the egg wash. If desired, sprinkle the top of the crust with sanding sugar.

Bake for 30 to 35 minutes, or until the crust is golden brown and the filling is bubbly. Allow to cool for 10 minutes before serving.

VANILLA BEAN TEA CAKES

Despite the use of the word "cake," tea cakes are a classic southern cookie. In my mother's old recipe collection, she had a couple of different recipes for tea cakes. I have tinkered with both of them, combined them a bit, and ended up happily with the version you see here. They're that perfect blend of slightly crispy around the edges and soft in the center. A big dose of vanilla is all the extra flavor you need for these beauties!

MAKES 30 COOKIES

2¾ cups (330 g) unbleached all-purpose flour

2 tsp (10 g) baking powder

½ tsp baking soda

½ tsp salt

¾ cup (170 g) unsalted butter, softened

1½ cups (300 g) granulated sugar

1 large egg

1 tbsp (15 ml) **vanilla bean paste**

½ cup (120 ml) **buttermilk**

Preheat the oven to 350°F (180°C). Line baking sheets with parchment paper or silicone liners.

Whisk together the flour, baking powder, baking soda and salt. Set aside.

Using an electric mixer on medium speed, beat the butter and sugar until light and fluffy. Add the egg and vanilla bean paste, and mix well.

Reduce the mixer speed to low. Add about a third of the flour mixture, and mix until a few streaks of flour remain. Mix in about half of the buttermilk. Add the remaining flour mixture in 2 portions, alternating with the remaining portion of buttermilk, mixing just until combined.

Drop the dough by 2-tablespoon (30-g) portions onto the prepared pans, leaving about 2 inches (5 cm) between the cookies. Bake for 15 to 18 minutes, or until the edges of the cookies are browned and the centers are set. Allow to cool on the pans on a wire rack for 10 minutes. Then transfer the cookies to the wire rack to cool completely.

TIP: Vanilla bean paste provides a visual appeal similar to that of vanilla beans but with a lower cost and without scraping vanilla beans. I just love seeing those little flecks of vanilla seeds in my baked goods!

HAZELNUT JAM BARS

These are the kind of sweet, fruity treats that are made for lunch boxes and afternoon snacks. Your favorite jam is sandwiched between layers of nutty shortbread. Lots of fruits lend themselves well to pairing with hazelnuts, but I'm especially fond of cherry and raspberry.

MAKES 24 BARS

FOR THE CRUST

2 cups (240 g) unbleached all-purpose flour

½ cup (100 g) firmly packed light brown sugar

½ tsp salt

1 cup (226 g) unsalted butter, cold, cut into small cubes

½ cup (60 g) **hazelnuts**, chopped

FOR THE FILLING

¾ cup (180 ml) **jam or preserves**

TO MAKE THE CRUST

Preheat the oven to 350°F (180°C). Grease a 9 x 13 x 2-inch (23 x 33 x 5-cm) baking pan.

Combine the flour, brown sugar and salt in a mixing bowl. Add the butter and mix with a pastry blender or a fork until combined. The dough will be crumbly, but it should hold together when pinched.

Set aside about a quarter of the crust mixture and place in a small bowl. Mix in the chopped hazelnuts.

Press the remaining dough firmly and evenly into the prepared pan.

TO MAKE THE FILLING

Gently spread the jam or preserves evenly over the crust. Sprinkle the reserved crust mixture over the top of the jam.

Bake for 30 to 35 minutes, or until the bars are golden brown. Allow to cool completely in the pan before cutting into bars.

LEMON GINGER SCONES

The zesty taste of ginger is a perfect pair for lemon. It adds a little bit of zing that somehow makes lemon even better. That flavor pair really shines in these scones, making them a great choice for a lazy weekend breakfast or for treating your guests to brunch.

MAKES 6 SCONES

2½ cups (300 g) unbleached all-purpose flour

¼ cup (50 g) granulated sugar

1 tsp (5 g) baking powder

1 tsp (2 g) ground ginger

½ tsp baking soda

¼ tsp salt

Zest of 1 medium **lemon**

½ cup (113 g) unsalted butter, cold, cut into small cubes

¾ cup (180 ml) **buttermilk**

Juice of 1 medium **lemon**

Sanding sugar (optional)

Preheat the oven to 400°F (200°C). Line a baking sheet with parchment paper or a silicone liner.

In a large mixing bowl, stir together the flour, granulated sugar, baking powder, ginger, baking soda, salt and lemon zest. Add the butter and mix with a pastry blender or a fork until the largest pieces of butter are the size of small peas.

Add the buttermilk and lemon juice, and mix until a dough forms. Transfer the dough to a lightly floured surface. Pat the dough into a circle about 7 inches (18 cm) in diameter. Cut into 6 wedges. Carefully transfer the wedges to the prepared pan, leaving about ½ inch (1 cm) between wedges. If desired, sprinkle with sanding sugar.

Bake for 18 to 22 minutes, or until the edges are golden brown. Allow to cool on the pan for 5 minutes before serving.

TIP: Sanding sugar is a coarse sugar that's often sprinkled on top of baked goods to give them a little extra bit of sweetness and a hint of sparkle. A package of it will last you quite a while and add a lovely finishing touch to baked goods, such as these scones.

DULCE DE LECHE SHORTBREAD BARS

I love the look of layered bars, such as these. The big secret here is that you can get that look without a lot of fuss. Just start by baking a simple shortbread crust, top that with rich dulce de leche and chocolate, and you're done. With a short baking time and a couple of quick refrigerator stints, you'll love how quickly and easily these bars come together.

MAKES 24 BARS

1 cup (226 g) unsalted butter, softened

¾ cup (150 g) firmly packed light brown sugar

1 tsp (5 ml) vanilla extract

2¼ cups (270 g) unbleached all-purpose flour

½ tsp salt

1 (13.4-oz [380-g]) can **dulce de leche** (see page 99)

9 oz (255 g) **semisweet chocolate**, roughly chopped

Preheat the oven to 350°F (180°C). Grease a 9 x 13 x 2-inch (23 x 33 x 5-cm) baking pan. Line the pan with parchment paper so that about 2 inches (5 cm) of paper hangs over the short ends of the pan.

Using an electric mixer on medium speed, beat the butter, brown sugar and vanilla until thoroughly combined.

Reduce the mixer speed to low. Gradually add the flour and salt, mixing just until combined.

Press the mixture firmly and evenly into the prepared pan. Bake for 20 to 25 minutes, or until the crust is golden brown. Set the pan on a wire rack, and allow the crust to cool to room temperature.

Spread the dulce de leche evenly over the cooled crust. Refrigerate for 20 minutes, or until set.

Place the chocolate in a microwave-safe bowl. Heat in a microwave at 50% power in 30-second increments until the chocolate melts when stirred. Stir until smooth. Allow to cool for 5 minutes. Then spread the melted chocolate evenly on top of the dulce de leche layer. Refrigerate for 20 minutes, or until set.

Use the overhanging parchment paper to lift the bars out of the pan and onto a cutting board. Use a sharp knife to cut into the bars.

BROWN SUGAR–CINNAMON BARS WITH NUTTY CREAM CHEESE FROSTING

One of the best things I've realized in my years of baking is that a dessert doesn't have to be overly complicated to be good. As a prime example, these bars are made with basic ingredients, yet have plenty of flavor. The addition of a sweet, nutty frosting is just the thing to make these bars simply delicious!

MAKES 16 BARS

FOR THE BARS

1 cup (120 g) unbleached all-purpose flour

1½ tsp (4 g) ground cinnamon

½ tsp baking powder

¼ tsp salt

½ cup (113 g) unsalted butter, softened

1 cup (200 g) firmly packed light brown sugar

1 large egg

½ tsp vanilla extract

FOR THE NUTTY CREAM CHEESE FROSTING

4 oz (114 g) **cream cheese**, softened

1 cup (200 g) firmly packed light brown sugar

¼ cup (57 g) unsalted butter, softened

½ tsp vanilla extract

¾ cup (90 g) **pecans**, chopped

TO MAKE THE BARS

Preheat the oven to 350°F (180°C). Grease an 8 x 8 x 2-inch (20 x 20 x 5-cm) baking pan.

Whisk together the flour, cinnamon, baking powder and salt. Set aside.

Using an electric mixer on medium speed, beat the butter and brown sugar until light and fluffy. Add the egg and vanilla, and mix well.

Reduce the mixer speed to low. Gradually add the flour mixture, mixing just until combined.

Spread the batter evenly in the prepared pan. Bake for 20 to 25 minutes, or until a pick inserted into the center comes out clean. Set the pan on a wire rack to cool completely.

TO MAKE THE NUTTY CREAM CHEESE FROSTING

Using an electric mixer on medium speed, beat the cream cheese, brown sugar, butter and vanilla until thoroughly combined. Mix in the nuts.

Spread the frosting evenly over the top of the cooled bars. Cut into squares and serve.

COCOA TOFFEE SHORTBREAD

One of the beauties of shortbread is its versatility. I enjoy experimenting with different flavor combinations and shapes to keep things interesting. This version highlights the rich complexity of cocoa powder and the sweet crunch of toffee.

MAKES 24 BARS

2 cups (240 g) unbleached all-purpose flour

3 tbsp (15 g) **unsweetened cocoa powder**

½ tsp baking powder

½ tsp salt

1 cup (226 g) unsalted butter, softened

⅔ cup (133 g) granulated sugar

½ cup (80 g) **toffee bits**

Grease a 9 x 13 x 2-inch (23 x 33 x 5-cm) baking pan. Line the pan with parchment paper so that the paper hangs over the short ends by about 2 inches (5 cm).

Whisk together the flour, cocoa powder, baking powder and salt. Set aside.

Using an electric mixer on medium speed, beat the butter and sugar until light and fluffy.

Reduce the mixer speed to low. Gradually add the flour mixture, mixing just until combined. Stir in the toffee bits.

Spread the dough evenly in the prepared pan. Refrigerate for 30 minutes.

Preheat the oven to 325°F (160°C). Bake the shortbread 25 to 30 minutes, or until set.

Place the pan on a wire rack and allow the shortbread to cool completely. Use the overhanging parchment paper to lift the bars out of the pan and onto a cutting board. Use a sharp knife to cut into bars.

APPLE PECAN TASSIES

When I met my husband, Quinn, I often unintentionally amused him with my use of southern colloquialisms. I remember baking a batch of mini pecan pies and referring to them as pecan tassies. He had never heard that term, and I was so surprised that a word I knew so well could be so foreign to him. Regardless of its regional origins, I still refer to little pies as tassies. It just seems like the perfect word for these mini treats. With this recipe, I took the idea of pecan tassies and added some elements of another classic pie with apples and cinnamon.

MAKES 24 TASSIES

FOR THE BASIC BUTTER PIE CRUST

1¼ cups (150 g) unbleached all-purpose flour

1 tsp (4 g) granulated sugar

½ tsp salt

½ cup (113 g) unsalted butter, cold, cut into small cubes

3 to 4 tbsp (45 to 60 ml) cold water

FOR THE FILLING

2 medium **apples**, cored and diced

3 tbsp (38 g) granulated sugar

1 tbsp (14 g) unsalted butter

2 tsp (5 g) unbleached all-purpose flour

1½ tsp (4 g) ground cinnamon

¼ tsp salt

½ cup (60 g) **pecans**, chopped

TO MAKE THE BASIC BUTTER PIE CRUST

Combine the flour, sugar and salt in a large bowl. Add the butter and mix with a pastry blender or a fork until the largest pieces of butter are about the size of large peas. Add the water, about a tablespoon (15 ml) at a time, and mix until a dough forms.

Shape the dough into a ball, place on a sheet of plastic wrap, and flatten slightly into a disk about 1 inch (2.5 cm) thick. Wrap the dough tightly in plastic wrap and refrigerate for at least 2 hours.

Preheat the oven to 400°F (200°C). Lightly grease 24 mini muffin cups.

Place the chilled dough on a lightly floured surface. Roll the dough into a circle ⅛ inch (0.3 cm) thick. Using a 2¼-inch (5.7-cm) cutter, cut the dough into 24 rounds. Fit the crusts into the prepared muffin cups. Gather the remaining dough and re-roll. Use a sharp knife to cut forty-eight 1¼ x ¼-inch (3 x 0.6-cm) strips for topping the pies.

TO MAKE THE FILLING

Combine the apples, sugar, butter, flour, cinnamon and salt in a medium saucepan or skillet. Cook over medium heat, stirring frequently, for 5 to 8 minutes, or until the sugar has dissolved and the mixture has thickened. Stir in the pecans.

Divide the filling among the pie crusts, filling to the top of the crusts. Top each with two pie crust strips.

Bake for 15 to 20 minutes, or until the crusts are lightly browned. Allow to cool in the pans for 10 minutes. Then transfer the pies to a wire rack to cool completely.

TIP: See page 16 for tips on choosing apples for baking.

CHAI SPICE BROWNIES

The first time I tried chocolate combined with chai spices, I confess that I was surprised at how much I liked it. In fact, I was so enamored that I knew I had to reproduce that amazing flavor. As I began researching chai spice blends, I found that there are many accepted variations. After settling on my favorite combination of spices, I added it to rich, fudgy brownies. These may look like standard brownies, but bite into one and let the flavor grab your attention and your taste buds!

MAKES 16 BROWNIES

6 oz (170 g) **bittersweet chocolate**, roughly chopped

½ cup (113 g) unsalted butter

1 cup (200 g) granulated sugar

2 large eggs

1 tsp (5 ml) vanilla extract

1 cup (120 g) unbleached all-purpose flour

½ tsp salt

½ tsp **ground cardamom**

¼ tsp ground cinnamon

¼ tsp ground ginger

¼ tsp ground black pepper

Preheat the oven to 350°F (180°C). Grease an 8 x 8 x 2-inch (20 x 20 x 5-cm) baking pan.

Place the chocolate and butter in a microwave-safe bowl. Heat in the microwave at 50% power in 30-second increments until the butter has melted and the chocolate melts when stirred. Stir until smooth. Set aside to cool slightly.

Combine the sugar, eggs and vanilla in a large mixing bowl. Add the cooled chocolate mixture, and stir until well combined. Add the flour, salt, cardamom, cinnamon, ginger and black pepper. Stir just until combined.

Transfer the batter to the prepared pan and spread evenly. Bake for 30 to 35 minutes, or until a pick inserted into the center comes out with moist crumbs. Allow to cool in the pan for 10 minutes before cutting into bars.

JAM HAND PIES

At any given time, there are likely numerous jars of fruit preserves and jams in my refrigerator.
They are one of my favorite baking ingredients because they are a great, simple way to add fruit to desserts.
With this recipe, your favorite jam serves as a simple filling for handheld pies. I like to sprinkle the tops of these little
beauties with a coarse sanding sugar for a little burst of sweetness as well as for the visual appeal.

MAKES 20 PIES

FOR THE CRUST

1 cup (226 g) unsalted butter, cold, cut into small cubes

8 oz (227 g) **cream cheese**, cut into small cubes and softened

2½ cups (300 g) unbleached all-purpose flour

2 tsp (8 g) granulated sugar

½ tsp salt

FOR THE FILLING

About ½ cup (120 ml) **jam or preserves**

1 large egg

1 tbsp (15 ml) water, plus more for brushing the crusts

Sanding sugar (optional) (see page 44)

TO MAKE THE CRUST

Place the butter, cream cheese, flour, granulated sugar and salt in the bowl of a food processor. Pulse until a dough forms, about a minute.

Divide the dough in half. Gather each portion of the dough into a ball and flatten to a disk about 1-inch (2.5-cm) thick. Wrap each portion in plastic wrap and refrigerate for 30 minutes.

Preheat the oven to 400°F (200°C). Line baking sheets with parchment paper or silicone liners.

Place the chilled pastry dough on a lightly floured surface. Roll the dough into a circle ⅛-inch (0.3-cm) thick. Use a 3-inch (7.5-cm) round cutter to cut the dough into rounds. Gather the remaining dough and re-roll as needed to make 40 rounds.

TO MAKE THE FILLING

Place half of the dough rounds on the prepared pans. Top each with about 1 teaspoon (5 ml) of jam, leaving about a ¼-inch (0.6-cm) border around the edges. Brush the outside edges lightly with water.

Use a knife to make a small slit in the top of the remaining dough rounds. Place each on top of a jam-covered dough round. Press the edges to seal.

In a small bowl, lightly beat the egg and water to make an egg wash. Brush the top of each pie with the egg wash. You won't use all of the egg wash. If desired, sprinkle each pie with about ¼ teaspoon of sanding sugar.

Bake for 15 to 20 minutes, or until golden brown. Allow to cool on the pans for 10 minutes. Then transfer the pies to a wire rack to cool completely.

TIP: This dough is one of my favorites because of how simple it is to make as well as how great it tastes. I generally prefer to make pastry doughs by hand, but this one mixes so beautifully in a food processor that I recommend you use that method if possible.

PISTACHIO CHEESECAKE

The thought of baking a cheesecake is intimidating to some people. I know because I used to be one of them.
But in all honesty, it's really one of the simplest things to make. No, really! They usually start with a basic crust,
and the filling is a short list of ingredients mixed in one bowl. See? Simple! This sweet, nutty cheesecake is even simpler
than usual. You won't even need a springform pan. Just a tart pan or even a pie pan will do. Simple crust, simple filling,
a sprinkling of pistachios, bake, chill and there you go. Cheesecake!

MAKES 8 TO 10 SERVINGS

FOR THE CRUST

1 cup (120 g) unbleached all-purpose flour

½ cup (100 g) firmly packed light
brown sugar

¼ tsp salt

½ cup (113 g) unsalted butter, cold,
cut into small cubes

¼ cup (30 g) unsalted **pistachios**, finely
chopped

FOR THE FILLING

8 oz (227 g) **cream cheese**, softened

½ cup (100 g) granulated sugar

1 large egg

1 tsp (5 ml) vanilla extract

6 oz (170 g) unsalted **pistachios**

TO MAKE THE CRUST

Preheat the oven to 350°F (180°C). Grease a 9-inch (23-cm) round tart pan with a
removable bottom.

Combine the flour, brown sugar and salt in a mixing bowl. Add the butter and mix with
a pastry blender or a fork until combined. The dough will be crumbly, but it should hold
together when pinched. Mix in the pistachios.

Press the crust mixture evenly and firmly in the bottom and up the sides of the prepared
tart pan. Place the pan on a baking sheet lined with parchment paper. Bake for 10 minutes.
Set aside to cool completely.

TO MAKE THE FILLING

Using an electric mixer on medium speed, beat the cream cheese, granulated sugar, egg
and vanilla until thoroughly combined and smooth. Pour the batter into the cooled crust.
Sprinkle the pistachios over the top of the filling.

Bake for 35 to 40 minutes, or until the filling is set. Allow the cheesecake to cool for
30 minutes. Then cover the cheesecake with plastic wrap or aluminum foil and place
in the refrigerator for at least 4 hours before serving.

+3 INGREDIENTS

Now we'll take things just one step further and add one more item to the shopping cart. With three additional ingredients, the recipes in this chapter will serve you well from breakfast to dessert. Apple Cinnamon Biscuits (page 104) will get your day off to a sweet start. Try Maple Nut Coffee Cake (page 108) or Peanut Butter Snack Cake (page 64) for an afternoon treat. Spiced Chess Pie (page 72) is the perfect end to your evening meal.

BLACK AND WHITE CHOCOLATE CHIP COOKIES

As much as we all love classic chocolate chip cookies, it's fun to add a little twist to them every once in a while.
These cookies are a mashup of chocolate chip cookies and chocolate–white chocolate cookies. Literally! These beauties
start out as one basic cookie dough. Then, simply divide the dough in half and create two versions.
Mash them together, and you've got two great cookies in one!

MAKES 30 COOKIES

2 cups (240 g) unbleached all-purpose flour

1 tsp (5 g) baking soda

½ tsp salt

1 cup (226 g) unsalted butter, softened

½ cup (100 g) granulated sugar

¼ cup (50 g) firmly packed light brown sugar

1 large egg

1 tsp (5 ml) vanilla extract

1½ tbsp (8 g) **unsweetened cocoa powder**

½ cup (85 g) **white chocolate chips**

½ cup (85 g) **semisweet chocolate chips**

Whisk together the flour, baking soda and salt. Set aside.

Using an electric mixer on medium speed, beat the butter, granulated sugar and brown sugar until light and fluffy. Mix in the egg and vanilla.

Divide the dough in half. Add the cocoa powder and white chocolate chips to one half of the dough, and mix just until combined. Mix the semisweet chocolate chips into the remaining half of the dough. Cover the mixing bowls with plastic wrap, and refrigerate the doughs for 1 hour.

Preheat the oven to 350°F (180°C). Line baking sheets with parchment paper or silicone liners.

Scoop about ½ tablespoon (7.5 g) of each dough and press together. Roll the combined doughs into a ball and place on the prepared pan. Flatten the cookie slightly. Repeat with the remaining dough.

Bake for 10 to 12 minutes, or until the edges of the cookies are lightly browned. Allow to cool on the pans for 10 minutes. Then transfer the cookies to a wire rack to cool completely.

PEANUT BUTTER SNACK CAKE

This a decidedly unfancy cake, but it is wonderfully flavorful and moist. It's the perfect kind of cake for serving straight from the pan. I like to make this cake to have around for an afternoon snack or a simple dessert option.

For a little added crunch, use crunchy peanut butter instead of creamy.

MAKES 16 SERVINGS

1½ cups (180 g) unbleached all-purpose flour

1 tsp (5 g) baking powder

½ tsp salt

½ cup (113 g) unsalted butter, softened

½ cup (128 g) creamy **peanut butter**

½ cup (100 g) granulated sugar

¼ cup (50 g) firmly packed light brown sugar

2 large eggs

1 tsp (5 ml) vanilla extract

½ cup (120 ml) **milk**

1 cup (170 g) **semisweet chocolate chips**

Confectioners' sugar (optional)

Preheat the oven to 350°F (180°C). Grease an 8 x 8 x 2-inch (20 x 20 x 5-cm) baking pan.

Whisk together the flour, baking powder and salt. Set aside.

Using an electric mixer on medium speed, beat the butter, peanut butter, granulated sugar and brown sugar until light and fluffy. Add the eggs, one at a time, mixing well after each addition. Mix in the vanilla.

Reduce the mixer speed to low. Add about a third of the flour mixture, and mix until a few streaks of flour remain. Mix in about half of the milk. Add the remaining flour mixture in 2 portions, alternating with the remaining portion of milk, mixing just until combined. Stir in the chocolate chips.

Transfer the batter to the prepared pan and spread evenly. Bake for 35 to 40 minutes, or until the edges are browned and a pick inserted into the center comes out clean. Allow to cool in the pan for 10 minutes before serving. If desired, sprinkle the cake with confectioners' sugar.

CINNAMON PEAR COBBLER

Fall has always been my favorite time of year. I welcome with open arms the cooler days, the changing leaves and the abundance of pears at the local markets. While others are clamoring for apples and pumpkins, I've mainly got my sights set on pears. One of my favorite ways to bake with pears is this simple cobbler. By first cooking the pears with a bit of brown sugar, butter and cinnamon, you'll create a caramel-like flavor that will really make this cobbler something special. Add a sweet, nutty topping, and you've got yourself a little bit of fall in a lovely dessert.

MAKES 6 TO 8 SERVINGS

FOR THE FILLING

5 or 6 medium **pears**, cored, peeled and chopped (about 3 cups [450 g])

¾ cup (150 g) firmly packed light brown sugar

2 tbsp (15 g) unbleached all-purpose flour

2 tbsp (28 g) unsalted butter, softened

2 tsp (5 g) ground cinnamon

FOR THE TOPPING

1 cup (120 g) unbleached all-purpose flour

½ cup (100 g) firmly packed light brown sugar

½ tsp baking powder

¼ tsp salt

½ cup (113 g) unsalted butter, cold, cut into small cubes

3 tbsp (45 ml) **milk**

½ cup (60 g) **pecans**, chopped

1 tbsp (12 g) turbinado sugar (optional)

Preheat the oven to 400°F (200°C).

TO MAKE THE FILLING

Stir together the pears, brown sugar, flour, butter and cinnamon in a skillet. Cook over medium heat until the sugar dissolves and the mixture is bubbly. Continue to cook for 5 minutes, or until thickened. Transfer the mixture to a 1-quart (1-L) baking pan.

TO MAKE THE TOPPING

Combine the flour, brown sugar, baking powder and salt. Add the butter, and use a pastry blender or a fork to mix until the largest pieces of butter are the size of small peas. Add the milk and mix just until combined. Stir in the pecans.

Drop the topping by spoonfuls over the filling in the pan. If desired, sprinkle the top with turbinado sugar.

Place the baking pan on a lined baking sheet to catch any spills. Bake for 30 to 35 minutes, or until the topping is brown and the filling is bubbly. Allow to cool for 10 minutes before serving.

TIP: Turbinado sugar is a large-crystal sugar that's brown in color. In this recipe, it's used much like sanding sugar for a bit of sweetness and sparkle.

PEANUT BUTTER BLONDIES WITH CHOCOLATE SHORTBREAD CRUST

Peanut butter and chocolate are a match made in dessert heaven. There's just something about all of that sweet, nutty and salty that makes them a perfect pair. I'm not sure I could ever tire of it. These bars combine a quick-mix chocolate shortbread crust with a peanut butter blondie studded with chocolate chips. A must-bake for peanut butter and chocolate fans!

MAKES 16 BLONDIES

FOR THE CHOCOLATE SHORTBREAD CRUST

¾ cup (90 g) unbleached all-purpose flour

⅓ cup (67 g) granulated sugar

¼ cup (20 g) **unsweetened cocoa powder**

¼ tsp salt

6 tbsp (84 g) unsalted butter, cold, cut into small cubes

FOR THE BLONDIES

1 cup (120 g) unbleached all-purpose flour

½ tsp baking powder

½ tsp salt

¾ cup (150 g) firmly packed light brown sugar

¼ cup (57 g) unsalted butter, melted and slightly cooled

¼ cup (64 g) creamy **peanut butter**

2 large eggs

1 tsp (5 ml) vanilla extract

½ cup (85 g) **semisweet chocolate chips**

TO MAKE THE CHOCOLATE SHORTBREAD CRUST

Grease an 8 x 8 x 2-inch (20 x 20 x 5-cm) baking pan.

Combine the flour, sugar, cocoa powder and salt. Add the butter and mix with a pastry blender or a fork until combined. The dough will be crumbly, but it should hold together when pinched.

Press the crust mixture into the bottom of the prepared pan. Chill for 30 minutes.

Preheat the oven to 350°F (180°C). Bake the chilled crust for 15 minutes. Set aside.

TO MAKE THE BLONDIES

Whisk together the flour, baking powder and salt. Set aside.

Using an electric mixer on medium speed, mix the brown sugar, butter and peanut butter until thoroughly combined. Add the eggs, one at a time, mixing well after each addition. Mix in the vanilla. Stir in the chocolate chips.

Spread the blondies evenly over the partially baked crust. Bake for 25 to 30 minutes, or until a pick inserted into the center comes out clean. Allow to cool in the pan for 10 minutes before cutting into bars.

CARAMEL POPCORN PEANUT BUTTER COOKIES

These cookies are just plain fun! Peanut butter, honey-roasted peanuts and caramel popcorn combine to create a cookie that is sweet, salty, crunchy and nutty all at the same time. Certain to spark some excitement, both kids and grown-ups will love this playful flavor combination.

MAKES 48 COOKIES

1½ cups (180 g) unbleached all-purpose flour

½ tsp baking soda

½ tsp salt

½ cup (113 g) unsalted butter, softened

1 cup (255 g) creamy or crunchy **peanut butter**

1 cup (200 g) firmly packed light brown sugar

1 large egg

1 tsp (5 ml) vanilla extract

1 cup (35 g) **caramel popcorn**, roughly chopped

½ cup (60 g) **honey-roasted peanuts**, chopped

Preheat the oven to 350°F (180°C). Line baking sheets with parchment paper or silicone liners.

Whisk together the flour, baking soda and salt. Set aside.

Using an electric mixer on medium speed, beat the butter, peanut butter and brown sugar until light and fluffy. Mix in the egg and vanilla.

Reduce the mixer speed to low. Gradually add the flour mixture, mixing just until combined. Stir in the popcorn and peanuts.

Drop the dough by tablespoonfuls (15 g) onto the prepared pans. Bake for 15 to 18 minutes, or until the cookies are lightly browned.

Allow to cool on the pan for 10 minutes. Then transfer the cookies to a wire rack to cool completely.

SPICED CHESS PIE

Sometime in my childhood, I declared chess pie to be my favorite pie. I really didn't know much about it other than the fact that I enjoyed eating it. Somewhere along the way in my adult life, I started baking all sorts of things and forgot about it. But after a long absence, that first bite was just as full of creamy, sweet flavor as I remembered. At its heart, chess pie is quite simple, both in ingredients and in preparation. This recipe is in keeping with that perfect simplicity but adds some wonderful flavor with a blend of spices.

MAKES 8 TO 10 SERVINGS

FOR THE BASIC BUTTER PIE CRUST

1¼ cups (150 g) unbleached all-purpose flour

1 tsp (4 g) granulated sugar

½ tsp salt

½ cup (113 g) unsalted butter, cold, cut into small cubes

3 to 4 tbsp (45 to 60 ml) cold water

FOR THE FILLING

1¾ cups (350 g) granulated sugar

½ cup (113 g) unsalted butter, melted and slightly cooled

3 large eggs

¼ cup (60 ml) **milk**

1 tsp (5 ml) vanilla extract

2 tbsp (18 g) **cornmeal**

½ tsp ground cinnamon

¼ tsp **ground allspice**

¼ tsp ground ginger

¼ tsp salt

⅛ tsp ground nutmeg

TO MAKE THE BASIC BUTTER PIE CRUST

Combine the flour, sugar and salt in a large bowl. Add the butter and mix with a pastry blender or a fork until the largest pieces of butter are about the size of large peas. Add the water, about a tablespoon (15 ml) at a time, and mix until a dough forms.

Shape the dough into a ball, place on a sheet of plastic wrap, and flatten slightly into a disk about 1 inch (2.5 cm) thick. Wrap the dough tightly in plastic wrap and refrigerate for at least 2 hours.

Place the chilled dough on a lightly floured surface. Roll the dough into a circle ⅛ inch (0.3 cm) thick. Transfer the dough to a 9-inch (23-cm) pie pan. Trim and crimp the edges as desired. Place the pie pan in the refrigerator while you prepare the filling.

TO MAKE THE FILLING

Preheat the oven to 325°F (160°C).

Place the sugar, butter, eggs, milk and vanilla in a large mixing bowl. Stir until thoroughly combined. Stir in the cornmeal, cinnamon, allspice, ginger, salt and nutmeg.

Transfer the filling to the crust. Bake for 55 to 60 minutes, or until the crust is golden brown and the filling is set. Allow to cool for 20 minutes before serving.

LEMON PISTACHIO CRESCENT COOKIES

Every holiday season of my childhood, my mother and I would bake cookies together. One of our favorites was a simple, nutty cookie made with a short list of ingredients. This cookie is a flavor twist on her recipe that I still love to bake, eat and share with friends and family. The sweetness and tartness of the lemon is a wonderful complement to the pistachios. These cookies have a lovely light texture. The outside is a bit crunchy, and the inside is so soft it melts in your mouth.

MAKES 36 COOKIES

2 cups (240 g) unbleached all-purpose flour

½ tsp salt

Zest of 1 medium **lemon**

1 cup (226 g) unsalted butter, softened

1 cup (110 g) **confectioners' sugar**, sifted, plus more for sprinkling on top of the cookies

Juice of 1 medium **lemon**

1 cup (120 g) unsalted **pistachios**, chopped

Preheat the oven to 350°F (180°C). Line baking sheets with parchment paper or silicone liners.

Whisk together the flour, salt and lemon zest. Set aside.

Using an electric mixer on medium speed, beat the butter, confectioners' sugar and lemon juice until light and fluffy.

Reduce the mixer speed to low. Gradually add the flour mixture, mixing just until combined. Mix in the pistachios.

Using about 2 teaspoons (10 g) of dough at a time, roll the dough into logs and bend each slightly to form crescents. Place the cookies on the prepared pans, leaving about 2 inches (5 cm) between the cookies.

Bake for 15 to 18 minutes, or until the edges are browned. Allow to cool on the pans for 10 minutes. Then transfer the cookies to a wire rack to cool completely. Sprinkle with confectioners' sugar.

FUDGY NUT TART

Everyone needs at least one super simple recipe in their dessert arsenal, and this is one of my favorites. The only baking involved is a short stint for the crust. That's topped with a rich chocolate filling made with just two ingredients. Some lightly salted mixed nuts top off this tart to create a terrific sweet and salty dessert. Then just let it chill for a bit and serve. No one will ever have to know how incredibly simple it is to make this beautiful dessert!

MAKES 16 SERVINGS

FOR THE CRUST

½ cup (113 g) unsalted butter, softened

½ cup (100 g) firmly packed light brown sugar

1 cup (120 g) unbleached all-purpose flour

½ tsp salt

FOR THE FILLING

14 oz (396 g) **sweetened condensed milk**

12 oz (340 g) **bittersweet chocolate**, roughly chopped

1 cup (120 g) lightly salted **mixed nuts**

TO MAKE THE CRUST

Preheat the oven to 350°F (180°C). Grease a 9- or 10-inch (23- or 25-cm) round springform pan.

Using an electric mixer on medium speed, beat the butter and brown sugar until light and fluffy.

Reduce the mixer speed to low. Add the flour and salt, and mix just until combined and the mixture forms crumbs.

Transfer the crust mixture to the prepared pan. Press evenly and firmly into the bottom of the pan.

Bake for 15 to 20 minutes, or until golden brown. Set aside.

TO MAKE THE FILLING

Place the condensed milk and chocolate in a heavy saucepan. Cook over medium heat, stirring frequently, for 8 to 10 minutes, or until the mixture is smooth and thickened.

Spread the filling evenly over the crust. Sprinkle the nuts over the top of the filling. Press down lightly. Refrigerate for at least 2 hours, or until the filling is set. Serve chilled or softened.

BROWNIE THUMBPRINTS

The pairing of chocolate and berries is a long-standing favorite. Here, basic brownies are baked in mini muffin cups for a little different presentation. Then simply make an indentation in the top of each and fill with a sweet, fruity filling.

MAKES 24 BROWNIES

FOR THE BROWNIES

6 oz (170 g) **bittersweet chocolate**, roughly chopped

½ cup (113 g) unsalted butter

1 cup (200 g) granulated sugar

2 large eggs

1 tsp (5 ml) vanilla extract

1 cup (120 g) unbleached all-purpose flour

¼ tsp salt

FOR THE FILLING

3 oz (85 g) **white chocolate**, roughly chopped

3 oz (90 ml) **strawberry or raspberry preserves**

TO MAKE THE BROWNIES

Preheat the oven to 350°F (180°C). Grease a 24-cup mini muffin pan.

Place the chocolate and butter in a microwave-safe bowl. Heat in a microwave at 50% power in 30-second increments until the butter has melted and the chocolate melts when stirred. Stir until smooth. Set aside to cool slightly.

Combine the sugar, eggs and vanilla in a large bowl. Add the cooled chocolate, and mix until smooth. Add the flour and salt, and mix just until combined.

Divide the batter among the prepared muffin cups, using about a tablespoon (15 g) of batter in each cup. Bake for 18 to 22 minutes, or until a pick inserted into the center of a brownie comes out with moist crumbs.

While the brownies are still warm, use the handle of a wooden spoon to make a ¼-inch (0.6-cm)-deep impression in the center of each brownie. Allow the brownies to cool in the pan for 10 minutes. Then transfer the brownies to a wire rack to cool completely.

TO MAKE THE FILLING

Place the white chocolate in a microwave-safe bowl. Heat in a microwave at 50% power in 30-second increments until the chocolate melts when stirred. Add the preserves and stir until thoroughly combined. Spoon the filling into the top of each cooled brownie.

BROWN BUTTER COFFEE CAKE WITH GRAHAM CRUMB TOPPING

Coffee cakes are one of my favorite things to bake. I love their texture, their flavors and their versatility.
It's hard not to love a cake you can justify eating for breakfast! One of the signature parts of a coffee cake
is its crumb topping. This one combines some usual crumb ingredients—brown sugar, nuts, cinnamon—with graham
cracker crumbs for a tasty twist on the classic. Add that crumb to a dense, delicious brown butter cake,
and you've got a coffee cake you'll find yourself craving morning, noon and night!

MAKES 16 SERVINGS

FOR THE TOPPING

⅓ cup (33 g) **graham cracker** crumbs

1 tbsp (12.5 g) firmly packed light brown sugar

½ tsp ground cinnamon

2 tbsp (28 g) unsalted butter, cold, cut into small cubes

⅓ cup (40 g) **pecans**, chopped

FOR THE CAKE

10 tbsp (141 g) unsalted butter, sliced

1¾ cups (210 g) unbleached all-purpose flour

1½ tsp (7.5 g) baking powder

½ tsp baking soda

½ tsp salt

¾ cup (150 g) granulated sugar

1 large egg

1 tsp (5 ml) vanilla extract

½ cup (114 g) **sour cream**

TO MAKE THE TOPPING

Combine the graham cracker crumbs, brown sugar and cinnamon in a small bowl. Add the butter and mix with a fork until crumbs form. Mix in the pecans. Refrigerate the topping while you make the cake.

TO MAKE THE CAKE

Preheat the oven to 350°F (180°C). Grease an 8 x 8 x 2-inch (20 x 20 x 5-cm) baking pan.

Place the butter in a medium, heavy saucepan. Cook over medium-low heat until the butter melts and begins to foam, about 3 minutes. Continue to cook, whisking occasionally, just until brown specks begin to form at the bottom of the pan and the butter has a nutty aroma. This should take only 2 to 3 minutes. Remove the pan from the heat and whisk lightly for about 30 seconds. Transfer the butter to a large mixing bowl and allow it to cool slightly. If desired, strain the butter to remove some of the browned bits.

Whisk together the flour, baking powder, baking soda and salt. Set aside.

Add the granulated sugar to the cooled brown butter, and mix until combined. Add the egg and vanilla, and mix well.

Add about a third of the flour mixture, and mix until a few streaks of flour remain. Mix in about half of the sour cream. Add the remaining flour mixture in 2 portions, alternating with the remaining portion of sour cream, mixing just until combined.

Transfer the batter to the prepared pan and spread evenly. Sprinkle the topping over the top of the batter. Bake for 30 to 35 minutes, or until a pick inserted into the center comes out clean. Allow to cool in the pan for 10 minutes before serving.

CHOCOLATE CHIP CREAM CHEESE BISCUITS

I don't know about you, but I'm all for finding ways to have chocolate for breakfast. These lightly sweet biscuits have bits of chocolate mixed right into the dough. One of these beauties warm from the oven is a fantastic treat!

MAKES 12 BISCUITS

2 cups (240 g) unbleached all-purpose flour

3 tbsp (37.5 g) firmly packed light brown sugar

1 tbsp (14 g) baking powder

½ tsp ground cinnamon (optional)

½ tsp salt

4 oz (114 g) **cream cheese**, cut into small cubes and softened

¼ cup (57 g) unsalted butter, cut into small cubes and softened

½ cup (120 ml) **milk**

½ cup (85 g) **semisweet chocolate chips** or chocolate chunks

Preheat the oven to 425°F (220°C). Line a baking sheet with parchment paper or a silicone liner.

Whisk together the flour, brown sugar, baking powder, cinnamon and salt. Add the cream cheese and butter, and use a pastry blender or a fork to combine. Mix until the largest pieces of butter are the size of small peas. Add the milk and mix just until a dough forms. Gently mix in the chocolate chips.

Transfer the dough to a lightly floured surface. Pat the dough into a circle about ¾ inch (2 cm) thick. Use a 2-inch (5-cm) round cutter to cut out the biscuits. Re-roll as needed and continue cutting out biscuits.

Place the biscuits on the prepared pan. Bake for 14 to 16 minutes, or until lightly browned. Serve warm.

SALTED BUTTERSCOTCH CHEESECAKE BARS

Butterscotch is one of my favorite flavors. It's hard not to love something made with brown sugar, butter and cream. Perhaps even better than butterscotch is salted butterscotch. Adding a bit of saltiness balances the sweetness and richness, and creates something pretty amazing. These simple cheesecake bars are swirled with homemade salted butterscotch to create a fabulous dessert. I prefer not to mix the butterscotch completely into the cheesecake filling, but rather stir it in with just a few turns so that you get little salty bites of it as you eat the bars.

MAKES 24 BARS

FOR THE SALTED BUTTERSCOTCH

1 cup (200 g) firmly packed light brown sugar

½ cup (113 g) unsalted butter, cut into 4 or 5 pieces

¼ cup (60 ml) **heavy cream**

1 tsp (5 ml) vanilla extract

1½ tsp (9 g) salt

FOR THE CRUST

2 cups (240 g) unbleached all-purpose flour

½ tsp baking powder

¼ tsp salt

1½ cups (120 g) **old-fashioned rolled oats**

½ cup (113 g) unsalted butter, softened

¾ cup (150 g) firmly packed light brown sugar

1 large egg

½ tsp vanilla extract

FOR THE FILLING

24 oz (680 g) **cream cheese**, softened

1 cup (200 g) granulated sugar

3 large eggs

1 tsp (5 ml) vanilla extract

TO MAKE THE SALTED BUTTERSCOTCH

Place the brown sugar and butter in a medium, heavy saucepan. Bring to a low boil over medium heat. Continue to cook, stirring frequently, until the mixture is smooth, about a minute. Continue to cook for 3 to 4 minutes, or until the mixture has thickened.

Remove the pan from the heat. Carefully add the cream (the mixture will bubble) and stir to combine. Stir in the vanilla and salt. Set the pan aside to allow the butterscotch to cool slightly.

TO MAKE THE CRUST

Preheat the oven to 350°F (180°C). Grease a 9 x 13 x 2-inch (23 x 33 x 5-cm) baking pan.

Whisk together the flour, baking powder and salt. Stir in the oats. Set aside.

Using an electric mixer on medium speed, beat the butter and brown sugar until light and fluffy. Add the egg and vanilla, and mix well.

Reduce the mixer speed to low. Gradually add the flour mixture, mixing just until combined. Press the crust mixture firmly and evenly into the prepared pan.

Bake for 10 minutes, or just until lightly browned. Set the pan aside while you make the filling.

TO MAKE THE FILLING

Using an electric mixer on medium speed, beat the cream cheese, granulated sugar, eggs and vanilla until thoroughly combined and smooth. Add the cooled butterscotch and stir 4 or 5 turns. You should see ribbons of butterscotch running through the batter.

Pour the batter over the partially baked crust. Bake for 50 to 55 minutes, or until the edges are browned and the center is set. Allow the bars to cool to room temperature. Then cover and refrigerate for at least 2 hours before cutting and serving.

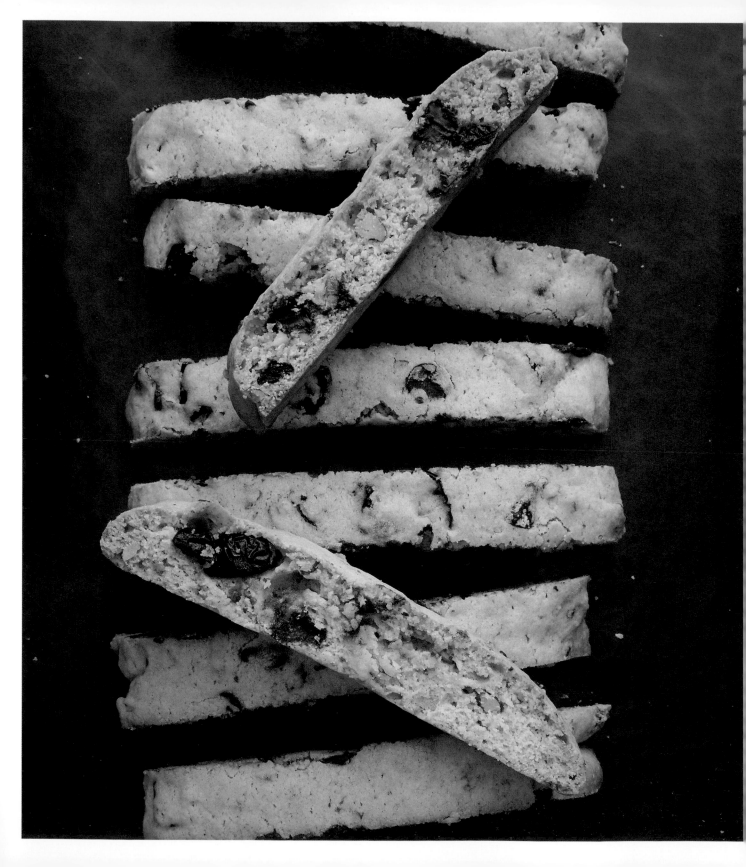

CRANBERRY CHOCOLATE PECAN BISCOTTI

Biscotti are one of those baked goods that look far more complicated to make than they really are. But the truth is that if you can make cookie dough, you can make biscotti. These crunchy cookies are a perfect companion for coffee, tea or even hot chocolate. Wrap up a batch of these for an excellent homemade gift for your family and friends.

MAKES 18 BISCOTTI

2 cups (240 g) unbleached all-purpose flour

1 tsp (5 g) baking powder

½ tsp salt

½ cup (113 g) unsalted butter, softened

½ cup (100 g) granulated sugar

¼ cup (50 g) firmly packed light brown sugar

2 large eggs

1 tsp (5 ml) vanilla extract

½ cup (85 g) **semisweet chocolate chips**

½ cup (60 g) **dried cranberries**

½ cup (60 g) **pecans**, chopped

Preheat the oven to 350°F (180°C). Line a baking sheet with parchment paper.

Whisk together the flour, baking powder and salt. Set aside.

Using an electric mixer on medium speed, beat the butter, granulated sugar and brown sugar until light and fluffy. Add the eggs, one at a time, mixing well after each addition. Mix in the vanilla.

Reduce the mixer speed to low. Gradually add the flour mixture, mixing until there are a few streaks of flour remaining. Stir in the chocolate chips, cranberries and pecans. The dough will be sticky.

Transfer the dough to the prepared pan. Dust your hands lightly with flour. Shape the dough to a 3½ x 15-inch (9 x 38-cm) rectangle ¾ inch (2 cm) thick. You may need to place the dough diagonally on the pan so that it fits better.

Bake for 25 minutes. Then remove the pan from the oven and allow the biscotti rectangle to cool for 10 minutes, or until it can be handled easily.

Use the parchment paper to lift the biscotti rectangle onto a cutting board. Cut crosswise into ¾-inch (2-cm) slices.

Place another sheet of parchment paper or a silicone liner onto the baking sheet. Place the sliced biscotti, cut side down, onto the pan. Bake for 18 to 22 minutes, or until lightly browned. Allow to cool on the pan for 10 minutes. Then transfer the biscotti to a wire rack to cool completely.

HAZELNUT MOCHA BROWNIES

Chocolate and coffee are a perfect match! Even if you aren't a coffee drinker, it's hard to argue
with the perfection of that combination. Add some hazelnuts, and you've got a wonderfully flavorful brownie.
These brownies can be whipped up and in the oven in short order. And all in one bowl, too!

MAKES 16 BROWNIES

6 oz (170 g) **bittersweet chocolate**, roughly chopped

½ cup (113 g) unsalted butter

1 cup (200 g) firmly packed light brown sugar

2 large eggs

1½ oz (45 ml) **brewed espresso or strong coffee**

1 tsp (5 ml) vanilla extract

1¼ cups (150 g) unbleached all-purpose flour

½ tsp salt

1 cup (120 g) **hazelnuts**, chopped

Preheat the oven to 350°F (180°C). Grease an 8 x 8 x 2-inch (20 x 20 x 5-cm) baking pan.

Place the chocolate and butter in a microwave-safe bowl. Heat in a microwave at 50% power in 30-second increments until the butter has melted and the chocolate melts when stirred. Stir until smooth. Allow the mixture to cool for about 10 minutes.

Add the brown sugar, eggs, espresso and vanilla to the cooled chocolate mixture. Stir until thoroughly combined. Stir in the flour and salt, mixing just until combined. Stir in the hazelnuts.

Transfer the batter to the prepared pan. Bake for 35 to 40 minutes, or until a pick inserted into the center comes out with moist crumbs. Allow to cool in the pan for 10 minutes before cutting into bars.

STRAWBERRY POT PIES

These beauties are a bit of a pie-cobbler hybrid. Like any good pie, they have a delicious filling and a flaky crust. But as with a cobbler, the filling is underneath the pastry. Instead of the mess you can get when you slice into a berry pie, you can embrace all that juicy, fruity filling when you dig in your spoon past the sweet crust.

MAKES 4 PIES

FOR THE CRUST

½ cup (113 g) unsalted butter, cold, cut into small cubes

4 oz (113 g) **cream cheese**, cut into small cubes and softened

1¼ cups (150 g) unbleached all-purpose flour

1 tsp (4 g) granulated sugar

¼ tsp salt

FOR THE FILLING

24 oz (680 g) **strawberries**, hulled

6 tbsp (75 g) granulated sugar

1 tbsp (8 g) **cornstarch**

1 tsp (5 ml) vanilla extract

1 large egg

1 tbsp (30 ml) water

1 tsp (4 g) sanding sugar (optional)

TO MAKE THE CRUST

Place the butter, cream cheese, flour, granulated sugar and salt in the bowl of a food processor. Pulse until a dough forms, about a minute. Gather the dough into a ball and flatten to a disk about 1 inch (2.5 cm) thick. Wrap the dough in plastic wrap and refrigerate for 30 minutes.

Butter four 4-ounce (118-ml) ramekins.

Place the chilled pastry dough on a lightly floured surface. Roll the dough into a circle ¼ inch (0.6 cm) thick. Use a round cutter to cut the dough into four rounds that will cover the top of the ramekins.

TO MAKE THE FILLING

Preheat the oven to 375°F (190°C).

Place about a third of the strawberries in a blender or food processor. Add the granulated sugar, cornstarch and vanilla. Blend until the strawberries are pureed. Transfer the mixture to a large bowl.

Cut the remaining strawberries into quarters. Add them to the pureed strawberry mixture and stir to combine. Divide the mixture among the prepared ramekins. Top each ramekin with a cut round of dough.

In a small bowl, lightly beat the egg and water to make an egg wash. Brush each crust lightly with the egg wash. You won't use all of the egg wash. If desired, sprinkle each pie with about ¼ teaspoon of sanding sugar.

Place the ramekins on a parchment-lined baking sheet to catch any spills. Bake for 25 to 30 minutes, or until the crusts are lightly browned.

TIP: The diameter of ramekins can vary, so you may not need all of the Cream Cheese Pastry Dough for making the crusts. If you have any leftover dough, use it to make some Jam Hand Pies (page 56).

TRIPLE CHOCOLATE CHUNK SKILLET COOKIE

Cookie dough is generally quick to make, but there are times that the thought of all that scooping dough and baking batches can make it seem like too much work. This big, flavorful cookie simplifies the entire process in a big way with the coveted trio of simple, quick and less mess. Every bit of the dough is mixed right in the pan, making for quick preparation and easy cleanup. Serve this one up warm from the oven. Add a few scoops of ice cream if you have some stashed in your freezer. Then just hand out the spoons, and watch it disappear!

MAKES 8 TO 10 SERVINGS

½ cup (113 g) unsalted butter, softened

1 cup (200 g) firmly packed light brown sugar

1 large egg

1 tsp (5 ml) vanilla extract

1¼ cups (150 g) unbleached all-purpose flour

½ tsp baking powder

½ tsp salt

½ cup (85 g) **semisweet chocolate chips**

½ cup (85 g) **milk chocolate chips**

½ cup (85 g) **white chocolate chips**

Preheat the oven to 350°F (180°C).

Place the butter in a 10-inch (25-cm) ovenproof skillet. Cook over medium heat until the butter has melted. Add the brown sugar and stir until the sugar dissolves. Remove the pan from the heat and allow the butter mixture to cool for about 10 minutes.

Add the egg and vanilla to the cooled butter mixture, and stir until combined. Add the flour, baking powder and salt, and mix just until combined. Stir in the chocolate chips. Spread the dough evenly in the skillet.

Bake for 15 to 20 minutes, or until golden brown. Serve warm.

ICED OATMEAL CUPCAKES

Remember iced oatmeal cookies? Those store-bought, crispy oatmeal cookies with a thin, sweet glaze on top?
I'm sure most of us had our fair share of those at birthday parties and in our school lunches. I know I did! These cupcakes
are an homage to those sweet cookies. The dense, oat-filled cupcakes are wonderfully hearty and delicious.
The sweet glaze is the perfect topping to create a delightful treat!

MAKES 12 CUPCAKES

FOR THE CUPCAKES

1½ cups (180 g) unbleached all-purpose
flour

1 tsp (5 g) baking soda

1 tsp (2.5 g) ground cinnamon

½ tsp salt

1 cup (80 g) **old-fashioned rolled oats**

½ cup (113 g) unsalted butter, softened

1 cup (200 g) firmly packed light
brown sugar

1 large egg

1 tsp (5 ml) vanilla extract

6 tbsp (90 ml) **milk**

FOR THE GLAZE

1 cup (110 g) **confectioners' sugar**, sifted

1 to 2 tbsp (15 to 30 ml) **milk**

TO MAKE THE CUPCAKES

Preheat the oven to 375°F (190°C). Grease 12 standard muffin cups.

Whisk together the flour, baking soda, cinnamon and salt. Stir in the oats. Set aside.

Using an electric mixer on medium speed, beat the butter and brown sugar until light
and fluffy. Add the egg and vanilla, and mix well.

Reduce the mixer speed to low. Add about a third of the flour mixture, and mix just
until there are a few streaks of flour remaining. Add about half of the milk, and mix until
combined. Alternate mixing in 2 more portions of the flour mixture with the remaining
milk. Mix just until combined.

Divide the batter among the prepared muffin cups, filling each about two-thirds full. Bake
for 12 to 15 minutes, or until a pick inserted into the center comes out clean. Allow to cool
in the pans for 10 minutes. Then transfer the cupcakes to a wire rack to cool completely.

TO MAKE THE GLAZE

Stir together the confectioners' sugar and 1 tablespoon (15 ml) of milk. If necessary, add
the remaining milk, a small amount at a time, until the glaze is the desired consistency.

Dip the top of each cooled cupcake into the glaze. Set the cupcakes on a cooling rack to
allow the glaze to set.

CRISPY OATMEAL COOKIES

Oatmeal chocolate chip cookies get a fun twist with the addition of crisp rice cereal.
That added crunch takes these cookies from ordinary to extra special.

MAKES 40 COOKIES

1 cup (120 g) unbleached all-purpose flour

½ tsp baking powder

½ tsp salt

2 cups (160 g) **old-fashioned rolled oats**

½ cup (113 g) unsalted butter, softened

½ cup (100 g) granulated sugar

¼ cup (50 g) firmly packed light
brown sugar

2 large eggs

1 tsp (5 ml) vanilla extract

¾ cup (128 g) **semisweet chocolate chips**

¾ cup (21 g) **crisp rice cereal**

Preheat the oven to 350°F (180°C). Line baking sheets with parchment paper or silicone liners.

Whisk together the flour, baking powder and salt. Stir in the oats. Set aside.

Using an electric mixer on medium speed, beat the butter, granulated sugar and brown sugar until light and fluffy. Add the eggs, one at a time, mixing well after each addition. Mix in the vanilla.

Reduce the mixer speed to low. Gradually add the flour mixture, mixing just until combined. Stir in the chocolate chips and cereal.

Drop the dough by tablespoonfuls (15 g) onto the prepared pans, leaving about 2 inches (5 cm) between cookies. Bake for 12 to 15 minutes, or until the edges of the cookies are browned.

DULCE DE LECHE MACAROONS

Macaroons are perhaps the ultimate in quick and easy cookies. Not only are they made with a short list of ingredients, but they're mixed entirely in just one bowl. You won't even need to get out the mixer for these. Just grab a spoon and stir!

MAKES 36 COOKIES

3 cups (360 g) **sweetened shredded coconut**

1 cup (120 g) **hazelnuts**, chopped

1 cup (300 g) **dulce de leche**

1 tsp (5 ml) vanilla extract

½ tsp salt

Preheat the oven to 350°F (180°C). Line baking sheets with parchment paper or silicone liners.

Stir together the coconut, hazelnuts, dulce de leche, vanilla and salt until thoroughly combined.

Drop the mixture by tablespoonfuls (15 g) onto the prepared pans. Bake for 12 to 15 minutes, or until the cookies are set. Allow the cookies to cool completely on the pans.

TIP: Dulce de leche is a sweet, thick sauce that is full of amazing caramel-like flavor. It can usually be found in the international foods section or the baking aisle of your local market.

COCONUT ALMOND BROWNIES

If you're a fan of the combination of chocolate, almonds and coconut, I'm guessing we have a favorite candy bar in common. Those flavors translate oh so well to brownies, too. These big, thick, fudgy brownies surround a sweet, nutty coconut filling for a brownie that will have you asking for seconds!

MAKES 16 BROWNIES

FOR THE BROWNIES

9 oz (255 g) **bittersweet chocolate**, roughly chopped

¾ cup (170 g) unsalted butter

¾ cup (150 g) granulated sugar

½ cup (100 g) firmly packed light brown sugar

3 large eggs

1 tsp (5 ml) vanilla extract

1¼ cups (150 g) unbleached all-purpose flour

½ tsp salt

FOR THE FILLING

¼ cup (57 g) unsalted butter

¼ cup (50 g) firmly packed light brown sugar

⅓ cup (40 g) **sweetened shredded coconut**

⅓ cup (40 g) **almonds**, chopped

Pinch of salt

TO MAKE THE BROWNIES

Preheat the oven to 350°F (180°C). Grease an 8 x 8 x 2-inch (20 x 20 x 5-cm) baking pan.

Place the chocolate and butter in a microwave-safe bowl. Heat in a microwave at 50% power in 30-second increments until the butter has melted and the chocolate melts when stirred. Stir well. Set aside to cool slightly.

In a large mixing bowl, stir together the granulated sugar, brown sugar, eggs and vanilla. Stir in the cooled chocolate mixture. Add the flour and salt, and stir just until combined.

Transfer all but about ½ cup (120 ml) of the batter to the prepared pan. Spread evenly.

TO MAKE THE FILLING

Place the butter and brown sugar in a medium saucepan. Cook over medium heat, stirring frequently, until the butter has melted and the sugar has dissolved. Stir in the coconut, almonds and salt. Continue to cook for 3 minutes to allow the mixture to thicken.

Drop the filling by spoonfuls over the batter in the pan. Drop the remaining brownie batter by spoonfuls over the filling.

Bake for 35 to 40 minutes, or until a pick inserted in the center comes out with moist crumbs. Allow to cool in the pan for 10 minutes before cutting into bars.

HONEY OAT PECAN BARS

These sweet, nutty bars are a bit of a twist on traditional pecan pie bars. The honey adds a nice sweetness and also helps thicken the topping. The oats provide a little bit of chewiness as well as some flavor.

MAKES 24 BARS

FOR THE SHORTBREAD CRUST

2 cups (240 g) unbleached all-purpose flour

½ cup (100 g) firmly packed light brown sugar

½ tsp salt

1 cup (226 g) unsalted butter, cold, cut into small cubes

FOR THE FILLING

¾ cup (150 g) firmly packed light brown sugar

¼ cup (57 g) unsalted butter, melted and slightly cooled

¼ cup (60 ml) **honey**

4 large eggs

2 tsp (10 ml) vanilla extract

¼ tsp salt

1½ cups (180 g) **pecans**, coarsely chopped

1 cup (80 g) **old-fashioned rolled oats**

TO MAKE THE SHORTBREAD CRUST

Preheat the oven to 350°F (180°C). Grease a 9 x 13 x 2-inch (23 x 33 x 5-cm) baking pan.

Combine the flour, brown sugar and salt in a mixing bowl. Add the butter and mix with a pastry blender or a fork until combined. The dough will be crumbly, but it should hold together when pinched.

Press the crust mixture firmly and evenly into the bottom of the prepared pan. Bake the crust for 15 minutes. Set aside to cool slightly.

TO MAKE THE FILLING

Mix the brown sugar, butter, honey, eggs, vanilla and salt until thoroughly combined. Stir in the pecans and oats.

Spread the filling evenly over the partially baked crust. Bake for 25 to 30 minutes, or until the filling is set. Allow to cool in the pan for 15 minutes before cutting into bars.

APPLE CINNAMON BISCUITS

Biscuits are one of my favorite breakfast treats, but there are times I want to skip the effort of rolling and cutting dough. That's when these biscuits are just the thing. The dough is mixed in one bowl, and the portions are simply dropped onto the baking pan. You can have these tasty biscuits mixed up and in the oven in short order.

MAKES 14 BISCUITS

2 cups (240 g) unbleached all-purpose flour

3 tbsp (37.5 g) firmly packed light brown sugar

2 tsp (10 g) baking powder

2 tsp (5 g) ground cinnamon

½ tsp salt

¼ cup (57 g) unsalted butter, cut into small cubes and softened

½ cup (114 g) **sour cream**

½ cup (120 ml) **milk**

1 medium **apple**, cored and diced

Preheat the oven to 375°F (190°C). Line a baking sheet with parchment paper or a silicone liner.

Combine the flour, brown sugar, baking powder, cinnamon and salt in a large mixing bowl. Add the butter and mix with a pastry blender or a fork just until combined. Stir in the sour cream and milk. This will form a sticky dough. Gently stir in the diced apples.

Drop the dough by 3-tablespoonful (45-g) portions onto the prepared pan, leaving about 2 inches (5 cm) between biscuits. Bake for 18 to 22 minutes, or until lightly browned. Serve warm.

TIP: See page 16 for tips on choosing apples for baking, such as Pink Lady, Fuji and Jonagold.

MINI STRAWBERRY BANANA BUCKLES

My husband's and my first New York apartment was close to a great coffee shop that served the most amazing individual fruit buckles. I don't drink coffee, but I frequently found myself stopping in for one of those buckles. With baking never far from my mind, I knew I just had to make my own little buckles. I added banana to the cake portion, topped it with strawberries and finished it off with a crumb topping. These are perfect for anything from breakfast to an afternoon snack to an after-dinner treat!

MAKES 12 BUCKLES

FOR THE CRUMB TOPPING

¾ cup (90 g) unbleached all-purpose flour

¼ cup (50 g) firmly packed light brown sugar

¼ tsp salt

¼ cup (57 g) unsalted butter, cold, cut into small cubes

FOR THE BUCKLES

2 cups (240 g) unbleached all-purpose flour

1 tsp (5 g) baking powder

¼ tsp baking soda

¼ tsp salt

½ cup (113 g) unsalted butter, softened

½ cup (100 g) firmly packed light brown sugar

2 large eggs

2 medium **bananas**, mashed

1 tsp (5 ml) vanilla extract

½ cup (120 ml) **buttermilk**

6 **strawberries**, hulled and chopped

TO MAKE THE CRUMB TOPPING

Combine the flour, brown sugar and salt in a small bowl. Add the butter, and mix with a pastry blender, a fork or your hands until crumbs form. Refrigerate the topping while you make the buckles.

TO MAKE THE BUCKLES

Preheat the oven to 350°F (180°C). Line 12 standard muffin cups with paper liners.

Whisk together the flour, baking powder, baking soda and salt. Set aside.

Using an electric mixer on medium speed, beat the butter and brown sugar until light and fluffy. Add the eggs, one at a time, mixing well after each addition. Mix in the bananas and vanilla.

Reduce the mixer speed to low. Add about a third of the flour mixture, and mix until a few streaks of flour remain. Mix in about half of the buttermilk. Add the remaining flour mixture in 2 portions, alternating with the remaining portion of buttermilk, mixing just until combined.

Divide the batter among the prepared muffin cups, using about 4 tablespoons (60 ml) per cup to fill each about three-quarters full. Top each with chopped strawberries. Sprinkle the crumb topping over the strawberries.

Bake for 25 to 30 minutes, or until a pick inserted into the center comes out clean. Allow to cool in the pans for 10 minutes before serving.

TIP: A buckle gets its name from what happens to the cake as it bakes. The weight of the fruit on top of the cake causes the center to sink, or buckle.

MAPLE NUT COFFEE CAKE

I spent many years thinking I didn't like maple syrup, not realizing that I had never had the real stuff.
Once I tasted real maple syrup, though, I definitely changed my tune. Now that big, rich maple flavor is one of my favorites!
Here, that amazing maple flavor combines with nuts and cinnamon to make a sweet, crunchy topping
for a classic coffee cake with a fresh twist.

MAKES 8 TO 10 SERVINGS

FOR THE TOPPING

1 cup (120 g) **nuts** (such as pecans, hazelnuts or almonds), chopped

3 tbsp (45 ml) pure **maple syrup**

½ tsp ground cinnamon

FOR THE CAKE

1¾ cups (210 g) unbleached all-purpose flour

1 tsp (5 g) baking powder

½ tsp baking soda

½ tsp salt

½ cup (113 g) unsalted butter, softened

½ cup (100 g) granulated sugar

¼ cup (50 g) firmly packed light brown sugar

1 large egg

1 tsp (5 ml) vanilla extract

⅔ cup (151 g) **sour cream**

TO MAKE THE TOPPING

Combine the nuts, maple syrup and cinnamon in a small bowl. Set aside.

TO MAKE THE CAKE

Preheat the oven to 350°F (180°C). Grease a 9-inch (23-cm) round or 8 x 8 x 2-inch (20 x 20 x 5-cm) baking pan.

Whisk together the flour, baking powder, baking soda and salt. Set aside.

Using an electric mixer on medium speed, beat the butter, granulated sugar and brown sugar until light and fluffy. Add the egg and vanilla, and mix well.

Reduce the mixer speed to low. Add about a third of the flour mixture, mixing just until a few streaks of flour remain. Add about half of the sour cream, and mix just until combined. Add 2 more portions of flour, alternating with the remaining portion of sour cream, and mix just until combined.

Transfer the batter to the prepared pan and spread evenly. Sprinkle the nut mixture over the top of the batter.

Bake for 35 to 40 minutes, or until a pick inserted into the center of the cake comes out clean. Allow to cool in the pan for 10 minutes before serving.

CHOCOLATE PECAN PINWHEELS

These fun pinwheels exist somewhere between pie and cookies. They eat like a cookie but are made with one of my favorite pastry doughs. A sweet chocolate and nut mixture fills a cream cheese pastry for a sweet treat that's as pretty as it is delicious.

MAKES 36 PINWHEELS

FOR THE CREAM CHEESE PASTRY DOUGH

1 cup (226 g) unsalted butter, cold, cut into small cubes

8 oz (227 g) **cream cheese**, cut into small cubes and softened

2½ cups (300 g) unbleached all-purpose flour

2 tsp (8 g) granulated sugar

½ tsp salt

FOR THE FILLING

¾ cup (75 g) firmly packed light brown sugar

½ cup (60 g) **pecans**, finely chopped

¼ cup (22 g) **unsweetened cocoa powder**

Pinch of salt

3 tbsp (42 g) unsalted butter, softened

TO MAKE THE CREAM CHEESE PASTRY DOUGH

Place the butter, cream cheese, flour, granulated sugar and salt in the bowl of a food processor. Pulse until a dough forms, about a minute.

Divide the dough in half. Gather each portion of the dough into a ball and flatten to a disk about 1 inch (2.5 cm) thick. Wrap each portion in plastic wrap and refrigerate for 30 minutes.

Place the dough on a lightly floured surface. Roll into a 9 x 14-inch (23 x 35-cm) rectangle ⅛ inch (0.3 cm) thick.

TO MAKE THE FILLING

Preheat the oven to 350°F (180°C). Line baking sheets with parchment paper or silicone liners.

Stir together the brown sugar, pecans, cocoa powder and salt. Add the butter and mix with a pastry blender or a fork until the mixture forms crumbs.

Sprinkle the filling mixture over the pastry dough. Starting with a long end of the pastry, roll the pastry toward the other long end to form a log. Place the seam side on the bottom. Use a sharp knife to cut the pastry into ¾-inch (2-cm) slices.

Place the slices, cut side down, onto the prepared pans. Bake for 20 to 25 minutes, or until the pastry is golden brown. Allow to cool completely on the pans.

CHOCOLATE PECAN BUNDT CAKE WITH SOUR CREAM GLAZE

The joy of a Bundt cake is that it's a beautiful cake without the fuss of frosting or even layering. This Bundt cake is delicious and dense. It's filled with fine pieces of chocolate and pecans. I use my food processor to make small pieces and little shards of chocolate and nuts, but you can also just chop them finely. Those little bits of chocolate and nuts distribute throughout the cake so that you get big tastes of each in every bite. The sweet glaze tops it off for a wonderful cake you'll find yourself making time and again.

MAKES 10 TO 12 SERVINGS

FOR THE CAKE

2 cups (240 g) unbleached all-purpose flour

1½ tsp (7.5 g) baking powder

½ tsp baking soda

½ tsp salt

1 cup (226 g) unsalted butter, softened

1 cup (200 g) granulated sugar

½ cup (100 g) firmly packed light brown sugar

3 large eggs

2 tsp (10 ml) vanilla extract

½ cup (114 g) **sour cream**

9 oz (255 g) **semisweet chocolate**, ground or finely chopped

6 oz (170 g) **pecans**, ground or finely chopped

FOR THE SOUR CREAM GLAZE

1 cup (200 g) granulated sugar

2 to 3 tbsp (28 to 42 g) **sour cream**

½ tsp vanilla extract

TO MAKE THE CAKE

Preheat the oven to 350°F (180°C). Generously grease a 12-cup (2.8-L) Bundt pan.

Whisk together the flour, baking powder, baking soda and salt. Set aside.

Using an electric mixer on medium speed, beat the butter, granulated sugar and brown sugar until light and fluffy. Add the eggs, one at a time, mixing well after each addition. Mix in the vanilla.

Reduce the mixer speed to low. Add about a third of the flour mixture, and mix until a few streaks of flour remain. Mix in about half of the sour cream. Add the remaining flour mixture in 2 portions, alternating with the remaining portion of sour cream, mixing just until combined. The batter will be thick. Stir in the chocolate and pecans.

Transfer the batter to the prepared pan and spread evenly. Bake for 45 to 50 minutes, or until a pick inserted into the center comes out clean. Allow to cool in the pan for 20 minutes. Then invert the cake onto a wire rack to cool completely.

TO MAKE THE SOUR CREAM GLAZE

Stir together the granulated sugar, sour cream and vanilla. Mix until smooth and pourable. Pour over the cooled cake.

+4 INGREDIENTS

Browse the recipes in this chapter, and you'll quickly see that adding four ingredients to your baker's pantry essentials can result in some fantastic treats. You'll also find that the addition of more ingredients doesn't have to equal more work. You can absolutely get big flavor with simple preparation.

Make the most of fresh berry season with Triple Berry Crumb Tart (page 133). Whip up a simple Weeknight Fudgy Brownie Cake (page 146) for a midweek treat. Make a weekend morning even better with a batch of Oats and Honey Scones (page 117) or Raspberry Gingersnap Muffins (page 145).

OATS AND HONEY SCONES

Scones are one of my favorite low-effort, high-reward breakfast treats to make. One mixing bowl, a bit of measuring and mixing, and a short oven time are all that you need to make a wonderful morning meal. The nuttiness and light sweetness of these scones make them a favorite with us. They are perfectly delicious on their own, but I often serve them with fruit preserves for a little extra flavor and sweetness.

MAKES 10 SCONES

1¾ cups (210 g) unbleached all-purpose flour

1 cup (80 g) **old-fashioned rolled oats**

2 tbsp (25 g) firmly packed light brown sugar

1 tsp (5 g) baking powder

¼ tsp salt

½ cup (113 g) unsalted butter, cold, cut into small cubes

½ cup (120 ml) **milk**

¼ cup (60 ml) **honey**

½ cup (60 g) **pecans**, chopped

Preheat the oven to 400°F (200°C). Line a baking sheet with parchment paper or a silicone liner.

Stir together the flour, oats, brown sugar, baking powder and salt. Add the butter, and mix with a pastry blender or a fork until the largest pieces of butter are about the size of small peas.

Add the milk and honey, and stir just until a dough forms. Gently stir in the pecans.

Drop the dough by ¼-cup (60-g) portions onto the prepared pan, leaving about 2 inches (5 cm) between the scones. Bake for 12 to 15 minutes, or until the scones are golden brown. Serve warm.

CARAMEL ALMOND CHOCOLATE CHUNK COOKIES

I've always been a sucker for giant cookies packed with lots of different additions. With so many tasty things packed inside them, no two bites are ever quite the same. These big cookies take traditional chocolate chip cookies and turn them into a big flavor experience with the addition of crunchy almonds, rich caramel and a bite of salt. I find that these cookies are best served warm so that the caramel is soft and a little gooey.

MAKES 16 COOKIES

3 cups (360 g) unbleached all-purpose flour

1 tsp (5 g) baking powder

½ tsp baking soda

½ tsp salt

10 tbsp (140 g) unsalted butter, softened

1 cup (200 g) granulated sugar

¾ cup (150 g) firmly packed light brown sugar

2 large eggs

2 tsp (10 ml) vanilla extract

¾ cup (128 g) **semisweet chocolate chunks** or chocolate chips

¾ cup (90 g) **almonds**, sliced

8 **soft caramels** (67 g), unwrapped and quartered

2 tsp (12 g) **coarse salt**

Whisk together the flour, baking powder, baking soda and salt. Set aside.

Using an electric mixer on medium speed, beat the butter, granulated sugar and brown sugar until light and fluffy. Add the eggs, one at a time, mixing well after each addition. Mix in the vanilla.

Reduce the mixer speed to low. Gradually add the flour mixture, mixing until there are still a few streaks of the flour remaining. Stir in the chocolate, almonds and caramels.

Cover the mixing bowl with plastic wrap, and refrigerate the dough for 1 hour.

Preheat the oven to 375°F (190°C). Line baking sheets with parchment paper or silicone liners.

Drop the dough by ¼-cup (60-g) portions onto the prepared pans. Flatten the top of each cookie slightly. Sprinkle the top of each cookie with coarse salt. Bake for 12 to 15 minutes, or until the cookies are lightly browned and set in the center.

Allow the cookies to cool on the pans for 10 minutes. Then transfer the cookies to a wire rack to cool completely.

CHERRY PISTACHIO MUFFINS

Muffins are one of the best grab-and-go breakfasts or snacks. I tend to like my muffins a little less sweet than the cakelike muffins you often find these days in bakeries and coffee shops. Instead, I like to focus on adding flavor with various add-ins. These simple muffins get their flavor from sweet, tart dried cherries and nutty pistachios.

MAKES 18 MUFFINS

2 cups (240 g) unbleached all-purpose flour

1½ tsp (7.5 g) baking powder

Zest of ½ medium **lemon**

½ tsp salt

½ cup (113 g) unsalted butter, melted and slightly cooled

1 cup (200 g) granulated sugar

2 large eggs

Juice of ½ medium lemon

1 tsp (5 ml) vanilla extract

½ cup (120 ml) **milk**

½ cup (70 g) **dried cherries**

½ cup (60 g) unsalted **pistachios**, chopped

Preheat the oven to 400°F (200°C). Line 18 standard muffin cups with paper liners.

Whisk together the flour, baking powder, lemon zest and salt. Set aside.

Stir together the butter, sugar, eggs, lemon juice and vanilla. Mix until thoroughly combined.

Add about a third of the flour mixture, and mix until a few streaks of flour remain. Mix in about half of the milk. Add the remaining flour mixture in 2 portions, alternating with the remaining portion of milk, mixing just until combined. Stir in the cherries and pistachios.

Divide the batter among the prepared muffin cups, using about 3 tablespoons (45 ml) of batter per cup.

Bake for 15 to 20 minutes, or until the edges are browned and a pick inserted into the center comes out clean. Serve warm.

BLUEBERRY HAZELNUT CRUMBLE

Summer can be a tough time to convince yourself to turn on the oven. But with the abundance of fresh berries, it's absolutely worth it to get the oven going for a fruity dessert. This crumble mixes up so quickly that I find myself turning to it often when I need a last-minute dessert. The flavor is amazing, too. The combination of sweet blueberries and crunchy hazelnuts is outstanding. Serve this crumble warm or chilled. A scoop of vanilla ice cream isn't a bad idea, either.

MAKES 8 TO 10 SERVINGS

FOR THE FILLING

3 cups (510 g) **blueberries**

¼ cup (50 g) granulated sugar

½ tbsp (4 g) **cornstarch**

½ tsp vanilla extract

FOR THE TOPPING

¾ cup (90 g) unbleached all-purpose flour

¾ cup (150 g) firmly packed light brown sugar

½ cup (40 g) **old-fashioned rolled oats**

⅔ cup (80 g) **hazelnuts**, chopped

¼ tsp salt

¼ cup (57 g) unsalted butter, cut into small cubes and softened

TO MAKE THE FILLING

Preheat the oven to 375°F (190°C).

Stir together the blueberries, sugar, cornstarch and vanilla. Transfer to a 2-quart (2-L) baking dish.

TO MAKE THE TOPPING

Stir together the flour, brown sugar, oats, hazelnuts and salt. Add the butter and mix with a pastry blender, a fork, or your hands until the mixture forms crumbs. Sprinkle the crumble mixture over the berry mixture.

Place the baking dish on a parchment-lined baking sheet to catch any spills. Bake for 35 to 40 minutes, or until the top is golden brown and the berry mixture is bubbly. Allow to cool for 10 minutes before serving.

CHOCOLATE OATMEAL CREAM PIES

These cookie sandwiches combine three of my favorite cookies into one. They are reminiscent of oatmeal cream pies with chewy oatmeal cookies surrounding a sweet filling. There is also some Oreo inspiration both visually and in taste. And there are even some elements of one of my favorite local bakery's chocolate whoopie pies that are filled with cream cheese frosting. All of that comes together for one sweet, chewy and absolutely delicious cookie treat!

MAKES 22 COOKIE SANDWICHES

FOR THE COOKIES

1¼ cups (150 g) unbleached all-purpose flour

¼ cup (20 g) **unsweetened cocoa powder**

½ tsp baking powder

½ tsp salt

3 cups (240 g) **old-fashioned rolled oats**

¾ cup (170 g) unsalted butter, softened

1 cup (200 g) granulated sugar

2 large eggs

1 tsp (5 ml) vanilla extract

FOR THE CREAM CHEESE FROSTING

6 oz (170 g) **cream cheese**, softened

6 tbsp (84 g) unsalted butter, softened

½ tsp vanilla extract

3 cups (330 g) **confectioners' sugar**, sifted

TO MAKE THE COOKIES

Preheat the oven to 350°F (180°C). Line baking sheets with parchment paper or silicone liners.

Whisk together the flour, cocoa powder, baking powder and salt. Stir in the oats. Set aside.

Using an electric mixer on medium speed, beat the butter and granulated sugar until light and fluffy. Add the eggs, one at a time, mixing well after each addition. Mix in the vanilla.

Reduce the mixer speed to low. Gradually add the flour mixture, mixing just until combined.

Drop the dough by tablespoonfuls (15 g) onto the prepared pans, leaving about 2 inches (5 cm) between cookies. Flatten each cookie slightly. Bake for 12 to 15 minutes, or until the cookies are set. Allow to cool on the pans for 10 minutes. Then transfer the cookies to a wire rack to cool completely.

TO MAKE THE CREAM CHEESE FROSTING

Using an electric mixer on medium speed, beat the cream cheese, butter and vanilla until smooth. Gradually add the confectioners' sugar, and beat until thoroughly combined and smooth.

Spread the frosting on the bottoms of half of the cookies. Top with the remaining cookies so that the bottoms of the cookies face each other and the frosting spreads to the edges.

LEMON-LIME BLONDIES

The fresh, bright flavors of citrus are on display with these blondies. These are far less gooey than traditional lemon bars. Instead, they are soft and sweet with just the right amount of citrus flavor. Almonds top off these bars for some crunch, and a sprinkling of confectioners' sugar adds a touch of sweetness to complement the tartness of the fruits.

MAKES 16 BLONDIES

1¼ cups (150 g) unbleached all-purpose flour

½ tsp baking powder

Zest of 1 medium **lime**

Zest of 1 medium **lemon**

½ tsp salt

½ cup (113 g) unsalted butter, softened

1 cup (200 g) granulated sugar

1 large egg

Juice of 1 medium **lime**

Juice of 1 medium **lemon**

½ cup (28 g) **almonds**, sliced

About ¼ cup (28 g) **confectioners' sugar**

Preheat the oven to 350°F (180°C). Grease an 8 x 8 x 2-inch (20 x 20 x 5-cm) baking pan.

Whisk together the flour, baking powder, lime zest, lemon zest and salt. Set aside.

Using an electric mixer on medium speed, beat the butter and granulated sugar until light and fluffy. Add the egg and mix well. Mix in the lime juice and lemon juice.

Reduce the mixer speed to low. Gradually add the flour mixture, mixing just until combined.

Transfer the batter to the prepared pan and spread evenly. Sprinkle the almonds over the top of the batter.

Bake for 25 to 30 minutes, or until a pick inserted into the center comes out clean. Allow to cool in the pan for 15 minutes before cutting into bars. Sprinkle the bars with confectioners' sugar just before serving.

STRAWBERRY PEANUT BUTTER SHORTCAKES

Strawberry shortcakes have been a fixture on summer tables for many, many years. It's such a simple yet delicious premise of combining biscuits or cake with fresh strawberries and whipped cream. As I was making a batch of biscuits one day, it occurred to me that peanut butter would be a great way to make those shortcakes even better. Now you can add a bit of peanut butter to the mix for a PB&J twist!

MAKES 8 SHORTCAKES

FOR THE BISCUITS

2¼ cups (270 g) unbleached all-purpose flour

2 tbsp (25 g) granulated sugar

1 tbsp (15 g) baking powder

½ tsp salt

6 tbsp (84 g) unsalted butter, cold, cut into small cubes

¼ cup (64 g) creamy **peanut butter**

½ cup + 2 tbsp (150 ml) **milk**

FOR THE STRAWBERRY FILLING

16 oz (454 g) **strawberries**, hulled and sliced or chopped

3 tbsp (38 g) granulated sugar

FOR THE SWEETENED WHIPPED CREAM

1 cup (240 ml) **heavy cream**

2 tbsp (25 g) granulated sugar

½ tsp vanilla extract (optional)

TO MAKE THE BISCUITS

Preheat the oven to 425°F (220°C). Line a baking sheet with parchment paper or a silicone liner.

Combine the flour, sugar, baking powder and salt in a large bowl. Add the butter, and mix with a pastry blender or a fork until the largest pieces of butter are about the size of small peas. Mix in the peanut butter and milk just until combined. Don't overwork the dough. If you can still see a few streaks of peanut butter, that's fine. Transfer the dough to a lightly floured surface. Pat the dough into a circle about ¾ inch (2 cm) thick. Use a 2-inch (5-cm) round cutter to cut out the biscuits. Re-roll as needed and continue cutting out biscuits.

Place the biscuits on the prepared pan. Bake for 14 to 16 minutes, or until lightly browned.

TO MAKE THE STRAWBERRY FILLING

While the shortcakes are baking, combine the strawberries and sugar, and set aside.

TO MAKE THE SWEETENED WHIPPED CREAM

Place the cream in a large mixing bowl. Using an electric mixer with a whisk attachment, beat the cream at medium-high speed until it begins to thicken. Sprinkle the sugar over the thickened cream and continue to mix until combined. Add the vanilla, and continue to beat until you can lift the whisk out of the whipped cream and a peak that curves downward forms in the cream.

Split each biscuit in half. Cover the bottom half of each biscuit with a few strawberries (and their juice) and top with a dollop of whipped cream. Place the other half of the biscuits on top, and finish with the remaining strawberries and whipped cream.

SNICKERDOODLE SANDWICH COOKIES

My love of cinnamon is a relatively recent development. I was never much of a fan of it in my childhood, but now I simply can't get enough! One of my favorite ways to bake with cinnamon is making snickerdoodles. I just love their soft texture and all that cinnamon surrounding them. These beautiful, delicious sandwich cookies combine classic snickerdoodles with a sweet cream cheese frosting that has been given a flavor boost with a bit of coconut. The combination of flavors and textures is pretty irresistible!

MAKES 22 SANDWICH COOKIES

FOR THE CINNAMON-SUGAR

¼ cup (50 g) granulated sugar

1 tbsp (7.5 g) ground cinnamon

FOR THE COOKIES

3 cups (360 g) unbleached all-purpose flour

1 tsp (5 g) baking soda

½ tsp ground cinnamon

½ tsp **cream of tartar**

½ tsp salt

1 cup (226 g) unsalted butter, softened

1 cup (200 g) granulated sugar

½ cup (100 g) firmly packed light brown sugar

2 large eggs

1 tsp (5 ml) vanilla extract

FOR THE COCONUT CREAM CHEESE FROSTING

6 oz (170 g) **cream cheese**, softened

6 tbsp (84 g) unsalted butter, softened

½ tsp vanilla extract

3 cups (330 g) **confectioners' sugar**, sifted

¾ cup (90 g) **sweetened shredded coconut**

TO MAKE THE CINNAMON-SUGAR

Combine the granulated sugar and cinnamon in a small, shallow bowl. Set aside.

TO MAKE THE COOKIES

Preheat the oven to 350°F (180°C). Line baking sheets with parchment paper or silicone liners.

Whisk together the flour, baking soda, cinnamon, cream of tartar and salt. Set aside.

Using an electric mixer on medium speed, beat the butter, granulated sugar and brown sugar until light and fluffy. Add the eggs, one at a time, mixing well after each addition. Mix in the vanilla.

Reduce the mixer speed to low. Gradually add the flour mixture, mixing just until combined.

Using a tablespoon (15 g) of dough at a time, roll the cookies into balls and then roll each in the cinnamon-sugar. Place the cookies on the prepared pans, leaving about 2 inches (5 cm) between cookies. Bake for 8 to 10 minutes, or until the cookies are lightly browned and set. Allow to cool on the pans for 10 minutes. Then, transfer the cookies to a wire rack to cool completely.

TO MAKE THE COCONUT CREAM CHEESE FROSTING

Using an electric mixer on medium speed, beat the cream cheese, butter and vanilla until smooth. Gradually add the confectioners' sugar, and beat until thoroughly combined and smooth. Stir in the coconut.

Spread the frosting on the bottoms of half of the cookies. Top with the remaining cookies so that the bottoms of the cookies face each other and the frosting spreads to the edges.

TRIPLE BERRY CRUMB TART

I am probably in the minority, but I am not a big fan of summer. I much prefer fall and even winter weather. But I must admit that I do love baking with fresh summer fruits. I am fortunate to live in an area with seemingly countless farmers' markets filled with beautiful local berries and other fruits. Seeing all that fresh fruit always inspires me to get baking. This sweet tart is a delicious celebration of summer berries. The combination of blueberries, strawberries and blackberries is one of my favorites, but you can certainly use your favorite medley or just choose one variety. It's so fun to let this tart change as the calendar progresses and different berries come into season!

MAKES 8 TO 10 SERVINGS

FOR THE BASIC BUTTER PIE CRUST

1¼ cups (150 g) unbleached all-purpose flour

1 tsp (4 g) granulated sugar

½ tsp salt

½ cup (113 g) unsalted butter, cold, cut into small cubes

3 to 4 tbsp (45 to 60 ml) cold water

FOR THE FILLING

16 oz (454 g) total of **blueberries, strawberries, blackberries**

2 tbsp (25 g) granulated sugar

1 tbsp (8 g) **cornstarch**

FOR THE TOPPING

¾ cup (90 g) unbleached all-purpose flour

½ cup (100 g) firmly packed light brown sugar

¼ tsp vanilla extract

Pinch of salt

5 tbsp (70 g) unsalted butter, cold, cut into small cubes

TO MAKE THE BASIC BUTTER PIE CRUST

Combine the flour, granulated sugar and salt in a large bowl. Add the butter and mix with a pastry blender or a fork until the largest pieces of butter are about the size of large peas. Add the water, about a tablespoon (15 ml) at a time, and mix until a dough forms.

Shape the dough into a ball, place on a sheet of plastic wrap, and flatten slightly into a disk about 1 inch (2.5 cm) thick. Wrap the dough tightly in plastic wrap and refrigerate for at least 2 hours.

Place the chilled dough on a lightly floured surface. Roll the dough into a circle ⅛ inch (0.3 cm) thick. Transfer the dough to a 9-inch (23-cm) round tart pan with a removable bottom. Trim the edges of the dough to fit the pan. Place the pan in the refrigerator while you prepare the filling.

TO MAKE THE FILLING

Combine the berries, granulated sugar and cornstarch in a large bowl. Set aside.

TO MAKE THE TOPPING

Preheat the oven to 350°F (180°C).

Combine the flour, brown sugar, vanilla and salt. Add the butter and mix with a pastry blender or a fork until large crumbs form.

Transfer the berry mixture to the chilled crust and spread evenly. Sprinkle the crumb topping over the berries.

Bake for 50 to 55 minutes, or until the crust is golden brown and the filling is bubbly. Allow to cool 15 minutes before serving.

BROWN SUGAR COOKIES WITH MAPLE FROSTING

With just some ingredients from your baker's pantry, you have everything you need to make these sweet, simple cookies. The flavor fun comes with the frosting. Maple syrup adds such a delicious sweetness to otherwise traditional cream cheese frosting. The combination of that rich, sweet flavor with the brown sugar cookies is just lovely.

MAKES 36 COOKIES

FOR THE COOKIES

2 cups (240 g) unbleached all-purpose flour

1½ tsp (7.5 g) baking powder

1 tsp (6 g) salt

¾ cup (170 g) unsalted butter, softened

1½ cups (300 g) firmly packed light brown sugar

1 large egg

1 tsp (5 ml) vanilla extract

FOR THE MAPLE CREAM CHEESE FROSTING

8 oz (227 g) **cream cheese**, softened

½ cup (113 g) unsalted butter, softened

6 tbsp (90 ml) pure **maple syrup**

2 cups (220 g) **confectioners' sugar**, sifted

36 **pecan** halves

TO MAKE THE COOKIES

Preheat the oven to 350°F (180°C). Line baking sheets with silicone liners or parchment paper.

Whisk together the flour, baking powder and salt. Set aside.

Using an electric mixer on medium speed, beat the butter and brown sugar until light and fluffy. Add the egg and vanilla, and mix well.

Reduce the mixer speed to low. Gradually add the flour mixture and mix just until combined.

Drop the dough by tablespoonfuls (15 g) onto the prepared pans, leaving about 2 inches (5 cm) between cookies. Flatten each cookie slightly.

Bake for 10 to 12 minutes, or until the edges are browned. Allow the cookies to cool on the pans on a wire rack for 10 minutes. Then transfer the cookies to the wire rack to cool completely.

TO MAKE THE MAPLE CREAM CHEESE FROSTING

Using an electric mixer on medium speed, beat the cream cheese, butter and maple syrup until smooth. Gradually add the confectioners' sugar, and beat until thoroughly combined and smooth.

Spread the frosting on top of each cookie, and top each with a pecan half.

BANANA COCONUT MUFFINS WITH MACADAMIA CRUMB TOPPING

Banana muffins are pretty much a baking requirement. I long ago lost count of how many batches I've made in my baking life. The sweetness and texture of bananas so easily lend themselves to muffins and other quick breads, that I find myself making them often. These banana muffins are certainly not lacking in the flavor department. First, there's plenty of sweet coconut mixed into the batter. Then macadamias add crunch and nuttiness to an otherwise simple crumb topping. The combination of flavors and textures is really quite delicious!

MAKES 18 MUFFINS

FOR THE CRUMB TOPPING

⅓ cup (40 g) **macadamias**, chopped

¼ cup (50 g) granulated sugar

¼ cup (30 g) unbleached all-purpose flour

2 tbsp (28 g) unsalted butter, softened

Pinch of salt

FOR THE MUFFINS

1¾ cups (210 g) unbleached all-purpose flour

1 tsp (5 g) baking powder

½ tsp baking soda

½ tsp salt

½ cup (113 g) unsalted butter, melted and slightly cooled

½ cup (100 g) granulated sugar

½ cup (100 g) firmly packed light brown sugar

1 large egg

1 tsp (5 ml) vanilla extract

3 medium ripe **bananas**, mashed

½ cup (114 g) **sour cream**

1 cup (120 g) **sweetened shredded coconut**

Preheat the oven to 375°F (190°C). Line 18 standard muffin cups with paper liners.

TO MAKE THE CRUMB TOPPING

Combine the macadamias, granulated sugar, flour, butter and salt until the mixture forms crumbs. Refrigerate while preparing the muffins.

TO MAKE THE MUFFINS

Whisk together the flour, baking powder, baking soda and salt. Set aside.

Combine the butter, granulated sugar, brown sugar, egg and vanilla until thoroughly mixed. Stir in the bananas and sour cream. Add the flour mixture and stir just until combined. Stir in the coconut.

Divide the dough among the prepared muffin cups, using about 3 tablespoons (45 ml) of batter to fill each cup about two-thirds full. Sprinkle about 2 teaspoons (10 g) of the topping on each muffin.

Bake for 28 to 32 minutes, or until a pick inserted into the center comes out clean. Allow the muffins to cool in the pans for 10 minutes. Then transfer the muffins to a wire rack to cool completely.

TIP: I find that this type of crumb topping mixes best by hand. Jump in there and get your hands dirty!

CRUNCHY OAT BARS

These crunchy, crispy bars are packed with oats and brown sugar. A simple chocolate and peanut butter topping adds just the perfect flavor finish, and a sprinkling of toffee bits on top adds a nice crunch. Quick to mix and bake, this is the perfect recipe for when you want to satisfy a sweet craving in a hurry.

MAKES 24 BARS

FOR THE BARS

½ cup (113 g) unsalted butter, softened

1 cup (200 g) firmly packed light brown sugar

1 tsp (5 ml) vanilla extract

2 cups (160 g) **old-fashioned rolled oats**

½ tsp salt

FOR THE TOPPING

6 oz (170 g) **semisweet chocolate**, roughly chopped

½ cup (128 g) creamy **peanut butter**

¼ cup (40 g) **toffee bits**

TO MAKE THE BARS

Preheat the oven to 350°F (180°C). Grease a 9 x 13 x 2-inch (23 x 33 x-5 cm) baking pan.

Using an electric mixer on medium speed, beat the butter, brown sugar and vanilla until light and fluffy.

Reduce the mixer speed to low. Add the oats and salt, and mix just until combined. Transfer the mixture to the prepared pan and spread evenly.

Bake for 15 to 20 minutes, or until set.

TO MAKE THE TOPPING

Place the chocolate and peanut butter in a microwave-safe bowl. Heat in a microwave at 50% power in 30-second increments until the chocolate has melted. Stir until smooth.

Pour the mixture over the baked bars and spread evenly. Sprinkle with toffee bits. Allow the bars to cool and the topping to set before cutting into bars.

BLUEBERRY PINEAPPLE CRISP

I must confess that the first time I heard someone extolling the virtues of the combination of blueberries and pineapple, I was skeptical. Sure, I love the flavor, of both, but I couldn't quite imagine the two together. But trust me when I tell you that it works wonderfully. And this quick and easy crisp is a tasty way to enjoy the pairing. This crisp is made even simpler with a two-ingredient topping. Crushed vanilla wafers and a bit of butter create a sweet, crunchy topping that adds a good dose of vanilla to this dessert.

MAKES 10 TO 12 SERVINGS

3 cups (510 g) **blueberries**

8 oz (227 g) **pineapple**, chopped

2 tbsp (25 g) granulated sugar

1 tbsp (8 g) **cornstarch**

7 oz (198 g) **vanilla wafers**, crushed

6 tbsp (84 g) unsalted butter, cut into small cubes and softened

Preheat the oven to 375°F (190°C).

Stir together the blueberries, pineapple, sugar and cornstarch. Transfer to a 2-quart (2-L) baking dish.

Combine the vanilla wafer crumbs and butter with a fork or your fingers, mixing until crumbs form. Sprinkle the crumbs over the top of the fruit mixture.

Place the baking dish on a baking sheet lined with parchment paper to catch any spills. Bake for 25 to 30 minutes, or until the top is lightly browned and the filling is bubbly.

CHEESECAKE BLONDIES

Cheesecake brownies were always my pick at those little cookie shops in shopping malls.
Forget the cookies, I had my eyes on that brownie with the vanilla cheesecake topping! Then one day it hit me
that reversing that concept would be a grand idea. Why not top a blondie with chocolate cheesecake? Ground almonds
add a nutty flavor to the blondie base. Then, a rich chocolate cheesecake layer goes right on top.
Sweet, rich, chocolaty and nutty are a winning combination!

MAKES 24 BLONDIES

FOR THE BLONDIES

1½ cups (180 g) unbleached all-purpose flour

½ cup (50 g) ground **almonds**

½ tsp baking powder

½ tsp salt

1 cup (226 g) unsalted butter, melted and slightly cooled

1 cup (200 g) granulated sugar

½ cup (100 g) firmly packed light brown sugar

2 large eggs

1 tsp (5 ml) vanilla extract

FOR THE TOPPING

8 oz (227 g) **cream cheese**, softened

¼ cup (50 g) granulated sugar

½ tsp vanilla extract

1 large egg

3 oz (85 g) **bittersweet chocolate**, melted and slightly cooled

3 tbsp (45 ml) **heavy cream**

TO MAKE THE BLONDIES

Preheat the oven to 350°F (180°C). Grease a 9 x 13 x 2-inch (23 x 33 x 5-cm) baking pan.

Whisk together the flour, almonds, baking powder and salt. Set aside.

Stir together the butter, granulated sugar, brown sugar, eggs and vanilla, and mix well. Add the flour mixture and mix just until combined.

Spread the mixture evenly in the prepared pan.

TO MAKE THE TOPPING

Beat the cream cheese, granulated sugar, vanilla and egg until well combined. Add the chocolate and cream, and mix until smooth.

Carefully spread the topping mixture evenly over the crust. Bake for 30 to 35 minutes, or until the topping is set. Allow to cool in the pan for 20 minutes. Then cover the pan loosely and refrigerate at least 2 hours before serving.

RASPBERRY GINGERSNAP MUFFINS

After I began my baking adventures, I gave up store-bought baked goods almost entirely. I bake enough that I usually have something in the kitchen for when a sweet craving strikes. But I do still like to incorporate some sweet, crispy packaged cookies into my baking. These muffins have gingersnap crumbs mixed right into the batter and are studded with sweet raspberries. The combination of sweet and spicy is just lovely.

MAKES 12 MUFFINS

1¼ cups (150 g) unbleached all-purpose flour

1 cup (80 g) **old-fashioned rolled oats**

¾ cup (150 g) granulated sugar

½ cup (70 g) ground **gingersnaps** (about 10 gingersnaps)

2 tsp (10 g) baking powder

½ tsp salt

½ cup (113 g) unsalted butter, melted and slightly cooled

½ cup (120 ml) **milk**

2 large eggs

1 tsp (5 ml) vanilla extract

6 oz (170 g) **raspberries**, chopped into bite-size pieces

Preheat the oven to 400°F (200°C). Grease 12 standard muffin cups.

Stir together the flour, oats, sugar, gingersnaps, baking powder and salt in a large mixing bowl.

In a separate bowl, whisk together the butter, milk, eggs and vanilla. Add to the flour mixture, and mix until there are a few streaks of flour visible. Gently stir in the raspberries.

Divide the batter among the prepared muffin cups, filling each about two-thirds full. Bake for 15 to 18 minutes, or until the edges are browned and a pick inserted into the center comes out clean. Allow to cool in the pan for 10 minutes. Then transfer the muffins to a wire rack to continue cooling.

WEEKNIGHT FUDGY BROWNIE CAKE

Baking a homemade dessert can seem like a tall order on most weeknights. But what better time to treat yourself to a bit of chocolate comfort? This is the kind of cake that you can whip up and get into the oven quickly. Set out your butter to soften when you get home, change into some comfy clothes, get a simple dinner started and then get baking. Your reward will be this chocolate cake that's so delicious all on its own that it doesn't need a frosting.

MAKES 8 TO 10 SERVINGS

1¼ cups (150 g) unbleached all-purpose flour

¼ cup (20 g) **unsweetened cocoa powder**

½ tsp baking powder

½ tsp salt

¼ tsp baking soda

½ cup (113 g) unsalted butter, softened

½ cup (100 g) granulated sugar

½ cup (100 g) firmly packed light brown sugar

2 large eggs

3 oz (85 g) **bittersweet chocolate**, melted and slightly cooled

1 tsp (5 ml) vanilla extract

¼ cup (57 g) **sour cream**

1 cup (170 g) **semisweet chocolate chips**

Preheat the oven to 350°F (180°C). Grease a 9-inch (23-cm) round cake pan.

Whisk together the flour, cocoa powder, baking powder, salt and baking soda. Set aside.

Using an electric mixer on medium speed, beat the butter, granulated sugar and brown sugar until light and fluffy. Add the eggs, one at a time, mixing well after each addition. Mix in the cooled bittersweet chocolate and vanilla.

Reduce the mixer speed to low. Add about a third of the flour mixture, and mix until a few streaks of flour remain. Mix in about half of the sour cream. Add the remaining flour mixture in 2 portions, alternating with the remaining portion of sour cream, mixing just until combined. The batter will be thick. Stir in the chocolate chips.

Transfer the batter to the prepared pan. Bake for 25 to 30 minutes, or until a pick inserted into the center comes out clean. Allow to cool in the pan for 10 minutes before serving.

TIP: To get this cake into the oven even more quickly, you can speed up the butter softening process by cutting it into small pieces. This increases the surface area of the butter exposed to the air, making it ready for the mixer quicker.

PEACH COBBLER BREAD PUDDING

I've never been much of a bread baker, despite how much I like eating it. Instead, I prefer to get my fresh bread from one of our local bakeries. One of my favorite ways to use bakery bread is to make bread pudding. This one celebrates one of summer's best desserts—peach cobbler. Fresh peaches, pieces of crusty bread and plenty of cinnamon all come together for a delicious twist on both classic bread pudding and peach cobbler.

MAKES 10 TO 12 SERVINGS

10 oz (284 g) **baguette**, cut into bite-size pieces

2 or 3 medium **peaches**, cut into bite-size pieces

3 cups (720 ml) **milk**

¾ cup (150 g) firmly packed light or dark brown sugar

4 large eggs, lightly beaten

2 tsp (10 ml) vanilla extract

2 tsp (5 g) ground cinnamon

1 tsp (6 g) salt

¼ cup (30 g) **almonds**, sliced

Butter a 9 x 13 x 2-inch (23 x 33 x 5-cm) baking pan or a 3-quart (2.8-L) baking pan. Place the pieces of baguette and peaches in the pan, and toss to combine.

In a large bowl, whisk together the milk, brown sugar, eggs, vanilla, cinnamon and salt. Pour over the bread and peaches, pressing the bread down into the mixture to moisten. Cover and chill for 1 hour or overnight.

Preheat the oven to 350°F (180°C).

Sprinkle the top of the bread pudding with the almonds. Bake for 45 to 50 minutes, or until a knife inserted into the center comes out clean. Serve warm.

CASHEW CAKE WITH BUTTERSCOTCH FROSTING

Cashews are too often overlooked in the dessert world. I love their nutty, sweet taste, and I think they are the perfect addition to so many sweet treats. Topping off this cake is a rich butterscotch frosting. While I try not to play favorites, this is one of my all-time favorite frostings.

MAKES 12 TO 16 SERVINGS

FOR THE CAKE

2¼ cups (270 g) unbleached all-purpose flour

1½ tsp (7.5 g) baking powder

½ tsp salt

½ cup (113 g) unsalted butter, softened

1 cup (200 g) firmly packed light brown sugar

½ cup (100 g) granulated sugar

3 large eggs

½ tsp vanilla extract

1 cup (240 ml) **milk**

¾ cup (90 g) unsalted **cashews**, chopped

FOR THE BUTTERSCOTCH FROSTING

1 cup (200 g) firmly packed light brown sugar

½ cup (113 g) unsalted butter, cut into 4 or 5 pieces

¼ cup (60 ml) **heavy cream**

½ tsp salt

1 tsp (5 ml) vanilla extract

3 cups (330 g) **confectioners' sugar**, sifted

2 to 3 tbsp (30 to 45 ml) **milk**

TO MAKE THE CAKE

Preheat the oven to 350°F (180°C). Butter two 9-inch (23-cm) round cake pans. Line each pan with parchment paper, and butter the paper. Whisk together the flour, baking powder and salt. Set aside.

Using an electric mixer on medium speed, beat the butter, brown sugar and granulated sugar until light and fluffy. Add the eggs, one at a time, mixing well after each addition. Mix in the vanilla.

Reduce the mixer speed to low. Add about a third of the flour mixture, and mix just until there are a few streaks of flour remaining. Add about half of the milk, and mix until combined. Alternate mixing in 2 more portions of the flour mixture with the remaining portion of milk. Mix just until combined. Stir in the cashews. Divide the batter evenly between the prepared cake pans, and smooth the tops. Bake for 25 to 30 minutes, or until a pick inserted into the center comes out clean. Allow the cakes to cool in the pans on a wire rack for 10 minutes. Then invert the cakes onto the wire rack, remove the parchment paper and allow to cool completely.

TO MAKE THE BUTTERSCOTCH FROSTING

Place the brown sugar and butter into a medium, heavy saucepan. Bring to a low boil over medium heat. Continue to cook, stirring frequently, until the mixture is smooth, about a minute. Continue to cook for 3 to 4 minutes, or until the mixture has thickened.

Remove the pan from the heat. Carefully add the cream (the mixture will bubble) and stir to combine. Stir in the salt and the vanilla. Set the pan aside to allow the butterscotch to cool to room temperature and to thicken a bit more.

Transfer the cooled butterscotch to a large mixing bowl. Add about ½ cup (55 g) of the confectioners' sugar. Using an electric mixer on low speed, continue to mix while gradually adding the remaining confectioners' sugar. Mix until thoroughly combined and smooth. Add about 2 tablespoons (30 ml) of milk and mix until combined. If necessary, mix in about a teaspoon (5 ml) of milk at a time until the frosting is the desired consistency.

Place one cooled cake layer on a serving plate. Spread about half of the frosting on the top of the cake, spreading just up to the edges. Place the other cake layer directly on top of the frosted layer. Spread the remaining frosting on top of the top layer of cake.

+5 INGREDIENTS

Despite the longer list of ingredients, all the recipes in this chapter are still simple to make.

Some of the longer ingredient lists are mostly comprised of flavor add-ins. Sweet and Salty Blondies (page 164) feature a slew of tasty additions, and Peanut Butter Turtle Cookie Cups (page 168) combine the amazing flavors of chocolate, caramel, nuts and peanut butter.

Combine some simple techniques and favorite flavors to make Black Bottom Coconut Pecan Pie (page 172) and Coffee Caramel Chocolate Poke Cake (page 179). They may take a bit more time, but the preparation is still simple. And you'll quickly see (and taste) that the results are worth that extra effort!

SALTY TRIPLE CHOCOLATE COOKIES

Be warned. These are some of the most decadent cookies you will ever make. There's just so much good stuff going on here. Three kinds of chocolate make these some serious chocolate cookies. Cream cheese adds flavor and also helps create a wonderfully soft texture. Then there's the coarse salt on top. That really pushes these over the top to a sweet, salty, rich, downright amazing cookie.

MAKES 24 COOKIES

2½ cups (300 g) unbleached all-purpose flour

¼ cup (20 g) **unsweetened cocoa powder**

1 tsp (5 g) baking powder

½ tsp salt

½ cup (113 g) unsalted butter, softened

8 oz (227 g) **cream cheese**, softened

1 cup (200 g) granulated sugar

½ cup (100 g) firmly packed light brown sugar

2 large eggs

6 oz (170 g) **bittersweet chocolate**, melted and slightly cooled

2 tsp (10 ml) vanilla extract

1 cup (170 g) **semisweet chocolate chips**

Coarse salt

Preheat the oven to 350°F (180°C). Line baking sheets with parchment paper or silicone liners.

Whisk together the flour, cocoa powder, baking powder and salt. Set aside.

Using an electric mixer on medium speed, beat the butter, cream cheese, granulated sugar and brown sugar until light and fluffy. Add the eggs, one at a time, mixing well after each addition. Mix in the melted chocolate and vanilla.

Reduce the mixer speed to low. Gradually add the flour mixture, mixing just until combined. The dough will be sticky. Stir in the chocolate chips.

Drop the dough by 3-tablespoon (45-g) portions onto the prepared pans, leaving about 2 inches (5 cm) between cookies. Dampen your fingers with a bit of water and flatten each cookie slightly. Sprinkle a pinch of coarse salt on top of each cookie. Bake for 12 to 15 minutes, or until the cookies are still slightly soft in the center. Allow to cool on the pans for 5 minutes. Then transfer the cookies to a wire rack to cool completely.

TIP: Coarse salt refers to flakes of salt that are larger than standard table salt. Because of the size of the flakes, the flavor is more pronounced when a bit of it hits your tongue. My pantry usually has both kosher salt and sea salt for finishing off desserts with a salty bite.

DATE NUT OATMEAL MUFFINS

These muffins have so much going on for them that it's hard to know where to start talking about them.
There's the cream cheese in the batter that makes them dense yet soft. There are the sweet dates, the crunchy nuts,
the hint of cinnamon. And don't forget the oats that add a bit of chewiness. For a special treat, spread
a little cream cheese on one of these muffins warm from the oven.

MAKES 12 MUFFINS

1½ cups (180 g) unbleached all-purpose flour

1 tsp (5 g) baking powder

½ tsp salt

¼ tsp ground cinnamon

1 cup (80 g) **old-fashioned rolled oats**

¼ cup (57 g) unsalted butter, softened

4 oz (114 g) **cream cheese**, softened

¾ cup (150 g) firmly packed light brown sugar

2 large eggs

1 tsp (5 ml) vanilla extract

½ cup (120 ml) **milk**

½ cup (75 g) **dates**, chopped

½ cup (60 g) **pecans**, chopped

Preheat the oven to 400°F (200°C). Grease 12 standard muffin cups.

Whisk together the flour, baking powder, salt and cinnamon. Stir in the oats. Set aside.

Using an electric mixer on medium speed, beat the butter, cream cheese and brown sugar until light and fluffy. Add the eggs, one at a time, mixing well after each addition. Mix in the vanilla.

Reduce the mixer speed to low. Add about a third of the flour mixture, and mix until a few streaks of flour remain. Mix in about half of the milk. Add the remaining flour mixture in 2 portions, alternating with the remaining portion of milk, mixing just until combined. Stir in the dates and pecans.

Divide the batter among the prepared muffin cups, filling each cup about two-thirds full. Bake for 18 to 22 minutes, or until a pick inserted into the center of a muffin comes out clean. Allow to cool in the pans for 10 minutes. Then, transfer the muffins from the pan to a wire rack to continue cooling.

VANILLA BEAN CAKE WITH BLUEBERRY WHIPPED CREAM

This is the kind of cake I want gracing my summer table. No fussy layers, no overwhelming flavors, just a lovely cake to cap off a summer meal. This cake's light texture and vanilla flavor make it the perfect vehicle for a light, fluffy, fruit-filled whipped cream. You won't believe how quickly this one will disappear!

MAKES 8 TO 10 SERVINGS

FOR THE CAKE

1½ cups (180 g) unbleached all-purpose flour

1 tsp (5 g) baking powder

½ tsp baking soda

¼ tsp salt

¼ cup (57 g) unsalted butter, softened

4 oz (114 g) **cream cheese**, softened

1 cup (200 g) granulated sugar

2 tsp (10 ml) **vanilla bean paste**

½ cup (120 ml) **milk**

3 large egg whites

FOR THE BLUEBERRY WHIPPED CREAM

1 cup (240 ml) **heavy cream**

2 tbsp (25 g) granulated sugar

¼ cup (60 ml) **blueberry preserves**

Blueberries, for garnish (optional)

TO MAKE THE CAKE

Preheat the oven to 350°F (180°C). Butter a 9-inch (23-cm) round cake pan. Line the bottom with parchment paper, and butter the paper.

Whisk together the flour, baking powder, baking soda and salt. Set aside.

Using an electric mixer on medium speed, beat the butter, cream cheese and sugar until light and fluffy. Mix in the vanilla bean paste.

Reduce the mixer speed to low. Add about a third of the flour mixture, and mix until a few streaks of flour remain. Mix in about half of the milk. Add the remaining flour mixture in 2 portions, alternating with the remaining portion of milk, mixing just until combined.

In a separate bowl, beat the egg whites at medium speed until stiff peaks form. Gently fold the eggs into the cake batter.

Transfer the batter to the prepared pan, and spread evenly. Bake for 30 to 35 minutes, or until a pick inserted into the center of the cake comes out clean. Allow the cake to cool in the pan on a wire rack for 10 minutes. Then invert the cake onto the wire rack, remove the parchment paper, and allow the cake to cool completely.

TO MAKE THE BLUEBERRY WHIPPED CREAM

Place the cream in a large mixing bowl. Using an electric mixer with a whisk attachment, beat the cream at medium-high speed until it begins to thicken. Sprinkle the sugar over the thickened cream and continue to mix until combined. Continue to beat until you can lift the whisk out of the whipped cream and a peak that curves downward forms in the cream.

Transfer about one quarter of the whipped cream to a small bowl. Add the preserves and mix well. Add the blueberry mixture to the remaining whipped cream and fold gently to combine.

Spread evenly over the top of the cooled cake before serving. If desired, top the cake with fresh blueberries.

BANANA CHEESECAKE MINIS

Much like banana pudding, these bite-size cheesecakes are a delicious blend of creamy dessert, bananas and vanilla. A whole vanilla wafer serves as a crust for these sweet little gems. That's topped with a rich, creamy, banana cheesecake filling. Garnish with whipped cream and nuts for a lovely mini dessert.

MAKES 24 CHEESECAKES

FOR THE CHEESECAKES

24 **vanilla wafers**

8 oz (227 g) **cream cheese**, softened

¼ cup (50 g) granulated sugar

1 medium **banana**, mashed

1 large egg

½ tsp vanilla extract

FOR THE SWEETENED WHIPPED CREAM AND TOPPING

½ cup (120 ml) **heavy cream**

½ tsp granulated sugar

¼ tsp vanilla extract (optional)

¼ cup (30 g) **pecans**, chopped

TO MAKE THE CHEESECAKES

Preheat the oven to 350°F (180°C). Grease a 24-cup mini muffin pan.

Place a vanilla wafer in the bottom of each muffin cup. Depending on how your pans taper, you may need to place the cookie upside down to fit into the cup.

Using an electric mixer on medium speed, beat the cream cheese, sugar, banana, egg and vanilla until thoroughly combined and smooth.

Divide the batter among the prepared muffin cups, filling each almost to the top. Bake for 18 to 20 minutes, or until the filling is set. Allow to cool in the pan for 20 minutes. Use a knife to loosen the cheesecakes from the edges of the pan. Carefully remove the cheesecakes from the pan. Cover and refrigerate for at least 2 hours.

TO MAKE THE SWEETENED WHIPPED CREAM AND TOPPING

Place the cream in a large mixing bowl. Using an electric mixer with a whisk attachment, beat the cream at medium-high speed until it begins to thicken. Sprinkle the sugar over the thickened cream and continue to mix until combined. Add the vanilla, if desired, and continue to beat until you can lift the whisk out of the whipped cream and a peak that curves downward forms in the cream.

Top each cooled cheesecake with about 2 teaspoons (10 ml) of whipped cream before serving. Sprinkle the chopped pecans on top of each cheesecake.

HUMMINGBIRD BARS

Hummingbird cake is a southern dessert that's been around for years. There are several theories on how it got its name, but all you really need to know is that it's filled with bananas, pineapple and nuts, and usually topped with cream cheese frosting. That magical combination of flavors is why it's long been one of my favorite cakes. These bars take the flavors of that cake and turn them into bar form. The texture is somewhere between banana bread and a dense cake. They're delicate enough to serve with a fork, yet sturdy enough to eat with your hands.

MAKES 24 BARS

FOR THE BARS

2¼ cups (270 g) unbleached all-purpose flour

1½ tsp (7.5 g) baking powder

½ tsp salt

¾ cup (170 g) unsalted butter, softened

1 cup (200 g) granulated sugar

½ cup (100 g) firmly packed light brown sugar

1 large egg

1 tsp (5 ml) vanilla extract

3 medium ripe **bananas**, mashed

8 oz (227 g) **crushed pineapple**, drained

1 cup (120 g) **pecans**, chopped

FOR THE CINNAMON CREAM CHEESE FROSTING

4 oz (113 g) **cream cheese**, softened

¼ cup (56 g) unsalted butter, softened

1 tsp (2.5 g) ground cinnamon

½ tsp vanilla extract

2 cups (220 g) **confectioners' sugar**

¼ cup (30 g) **pecans**, chopped

TO MAKE THE BARS

Preheat the oven to 350°F (180°C). Grease a 9 x 13 x 2-inch (23 x 33 x 5-cm) baking pan.

Whisk together the flour, baking powder and salt. Set aside.

Using an electric mixer on medium speed, beat the butter, granulated sugar and brown sugar until light and fluffy. Add the egg and vanilla, and mix well. Mix in the bananas and pineapple.

Reduce the mixer speed to low. Gradually add the flour mixture, mixing just until combined. Stir in the pecans.

Spread the mixture evenly in the prepared pan. Bake for 40 to 45 minutes, or until a pick inserted into the center comes out clean. Set the pan on a wire rack to cool completely.

TO MAKE THE CINNAMON CREAM CHEESE FROSTING

Using an electric mixer on medium speed, beat the cream cheese, butter, cinnamon and vanilla until thoroughly combined. Gradually add the confectioners' sugar, and mix until smooth.

Spread the frosting evenly over the top of the cooled bars. Sprinkle the top with pecans, and cut into bars.

SWEET AND SALTY BLONDIES

Adding a little salty to your sweet can make magical things happen. These blondies are packed with a tasty combination of sweet and salty favorites—chocolate, nuts, chips, toffee and pretzels. If you're a big sweet and salty fan, sprinkle a little coarse salt on top of these bars before baking them. You'll get an even bigger salty bite!

MAKES 24 BLONDIES

2¼ cups (270 g) unbleached all-purpose flour

1 tsp (5 g) baking powder

½ tsp salt

1 cup (226 g) unsalted butter, softened

1½ cups (300 g) firmly packed light brown sugar

2 large eggs

1 tsp (5 ml) vanilla extract

½ cup (85 g) **semisweet chocolate chips**

½ cup (80 g) **pretzels**, crumbled

½ cup (60 g) **nuts** (such as pecans, almonds or walnuts), chopped

½ cup (42 g) **potato chips**, crumbled

¼ cup (40 g) **toffee bits**

Coarse salt (optional)

Preheat the oven to 350°F (180°C). Grease a 9 x 13 x 2-inch (23 x 33 x 5-cm) baking pan.

Whisk together the flour, baking powder and salt. Set aside.

Using an electric mixer on medium speed, beat the butter and brown sugar until light and fluffy. Add the eggs, one at a time, mixing well after each addition. Mix in the vanilla.

Reduce the mixer speed to low. Gradually add the flour mixture, mixing just until combined. Stir in the chocolate chips, pretzels, nuts, potato chips and toffee bits.

Transfer the batter to the prepared pan and spread evenly. If desired, sprinkle the top lightly with coarse salt. Bake for 28 to 32 minutes, or until a pick inserted into the center comes out clean. Allow to cool in the pan for 15 minutes before cutting into bars.

COCONUT BUNDT CAKE WITH RASPBERRY GLAZE

Coconut can be a polarizing ingredient. It seems people either love it or hate it. I am firmly on the pro-coconut side, never turning away any kind of coconut dessert. I am particularly fond of coconut combined with fruit flavors. This gorgeous cake is packed with plenty of coconut and topped with a simple raspberry glaze. For a little variety, try a different flavor, such as strawberry or cherry, for the glaze.

MAKES 12 TO 16 SERVINGS

FOR THE CAKE

3 cups (360 g) unbleached all-purpose flour

1½ tsp (7.5 g) baking powder

½ tsp baking soda

½ tsp salt

1 cup (226 g) unsalted butter, softened

2 cups (400 g) granulated sugar

3 large eggs

1 tsp (5 ml) vanilla extract

1 cup (240 ml) **buttermilk**

1½ cups (180 g) **sweetened shredded coconut**

FOR THE RASPBERRY GLAZE

1½ cups (165 g) **confectioners' sugar**, sifted

2 tbsp (30 ml) **milk**

2 tbsp (30 ml) **raspberry preserves**

FOR THE TOASTED COCONUT

Coconut, for garnish

TO MAKE THE CAKE

Preheat the oven to 350°F (180°C). Generously grease a 10- or 12-cup (2.4- or 2.8-L) Bundt pan.

Whisk together the flour, baking powder, baking soda and salt. Set aside.

Using an electric mixer on medium speed, beat the butter and granulated sugar until light and fluffy. Add the eggs, one at a time, mixing well after each addition. Mix in the vanilla.

Reduce the mixer speed to low. Add about a third of the flour mixture, and mix just until there are a few streaks of flour remaining. Add about half of the buttermilk, and mix until combined. Alternate mixing in 2 more portions of the flour mixture with the remaining portion of buttermilk. Mix just until combined. Stir in the coconut.

Transfer the batter to the prepared pan and smooth the top evenly. Bake for 50 to 55 minutes, or until a pick inserted into the center of the cake comes out clean. Allow to cool in the pan for 15 minutes. Then invert the pan onto a wire rack and allow the cake to finish cooling.

TO MAKE THE RASPBERRY GLAZE

Combine the confectioners' sugar, milk and preserves until thoroughly combined and pourable.

Pour the glaze over the cake before serving.

TO MAKE THE TOASTED COCONUT

If desired, you can garnish the cake with ¼ cup (30 g) of toasted coconut. To do so, spread the coconut in a single layer on a lined baking sheet. Bake at 350°F (180°C) for about 10 minutes, or until browned. Be sure to stir the coconut every few minutes to prevent burning.

PEANUT BUTTER TURTLE COOKIE CUPS

Turtle desserts have long been a favorite with me. The combination of chocolate, caramel and pecans is nothing short of fantastic. These little cookie cups make the turtle combo even better with the addition of peanut butter.

The only baking required here is for the cookie cups. Store-bought soft caramels combine with cream for a simple caramel filling for the cookies. Then, just top with melted chocolate and pecans, and you've created one delicious, gooey dessert!

MAKES 12 COOKIE CUPS

½ cup (113 g) unsalted butter, softened

1 cup (200 g) firmly packed light brown sugar

1 large egg

1 tsp (5 ml) vanilla extract

1 cup (255 g) creamy **peanut butter**

1½ cups (180 g) unbleached all-purpose flour

½ tsp salt

4 oz (114 g) **soft caramels** (about 15 pieces)

3 tbsp (45 ml) **heavy cream**

6 oz (170 g) **semisweet chocolate**, roughly chopped

12 **pecan halves**

Preheat the oven to 350°F (180°C). Grease 12 standard muffin cups.

Using an electric mixer on medium speed, beat the butter and brown sugar until light and fluffy. Add the egg and vanilla, and mix well. Mix in the peanut butter.

Reduce the mixer speed to low. Add the flour and salt, and mix just until combined.

Divide the dough among the prepared muffin cups, using about 3 tablespoons (45 g) of dough per muffin cup. Press the dough into the bottom and up the sides of each cup. Bake for 15 to 20 minutes, or until the cookies are lightly browned. After the cookies are baked, you may need to use a spoon handle or a tart tamper to re-shape them into cups. Set aside to cool slightly.

Place the caramels and cream in a microwave-safe bowl. Heat in a microwave at full power in 30-second increments until the caramels are melted. Stir until smooth. Spoon the caramel mixture into the cookie cups. Refrigerate the cookies while you prepare the chocolate topping.

Place the chocolate in a microwave-safe bowl. Heat in a microwave at 50% power in 30-second intervals until the chocolate melts when stirred. Stir until smooth. Top each cookie cup with melted chocolate. Place a pecan half on top of each cookie cup. Allow the chocolate to set before serving. Carefully remove the cookies from the pan and place them on a serving tray or a plate.

BLACK AND BLUE CHEESECAKE

I have always had a weakness for cheesecake, going back to when my mother would make them from box mixes. And I must say that homemade cheesecakes are much tastier and also surprisingly easy to make. At its heart, this is a very simple cheesecake made with a traditional graham cracker crust and a creamy filling lightly flavored with lemon. The big burst of flavor comes from that gorgeous berry sauce on top.

MAKES 16 SERVINGS

FOR THE CRUST

7 oz (200 g) **graham crackers**, finely crumbled

¼ cup (56 g) unsalted butter, melted

FOR THE FILLING

24 oz (680 g) **cream cheese**, softened

1 cup (200 g) granulated sugar

3 large eggs

Juice of ½ medium **lemon** (Be sure to save the zest for the topping.)

FOR THE TOPPING

3 oz (85 g) **blackberries**

3 oz (85 g) **blueberries**

3 tbsp (38 g) granulated sugar

3 tbsp (45 ml) water

½ tsp vanilla extract

Zest of ½ medium **lemon**

TIP: This method for baking has proven over the years to be a crackproof technique. It's far simpler than using a water bath. You'll just need to babysit the cheesecake for a while, so make sure you've planned ahead for the time required to get your perfect cheesecake.

TO MAKE THE CRUST

Preheat the oven to 350°F (180°C). Lightly grease a 9- or 10-inch (23- or 25-cm) round springform pan.

Combine graham cracker crumbs and butter until the crumbs are thoroughly moistened. Press the mixture evenly and firmly into the bottom of the prepared pan. Place the pan on a baking sheet lined with parchment paper to make it simpler to get in and out of the oven and to catch any potential leaks. Bake for 15 minutes, or until the crust is lightly browned. Then set the pan on a wire rack to cool slightly.

TO MAKE THE FILLING

Using an electric mixer on medium speed, beat the cream cheese and sugar until combined. Add the eggs and lemon juice, and mix until smooth. Pour the filling on top of the cooled crust and spread evenly. Bake for 15 minutes. Then, reduce the oven temperature to 200°F (93°C). Bake the cheesecake for 2 hours, or just until set.

Turn off the oven. Remove the cheesecake from the oven and carefully run a thin knife around the edge. Return the cheesecake to the oven. Leave the cheesecake in the oven for 2 hours. Then remove from the oven, cover loosely with plastic wrap, and refrigerate for at least 8 hours.

TO MAKE THE TOPPING

Combine the blackberries, blueberries, sugar and water in a heavy saucepan. Bring the mixture to a simmer over medium heat. Cook, stirring occasionally, for 5 to 8 minutes, or until the sugar has dissolved and the berries begin to break apart.

Remove the pan from the heat and stir in the vanilla and lemon zest. Allow the topping to cool to room temperature. It will thicken a bit as it cools. Remove the sides of the springform pan and top the cheesecake or individual slices with the cooled topping when serving.

BLACK BOTTOM COCONUT PECAN PIE

Pecan pie is one of my all-time favorite desserts. And it seems I'm always trying to think of new twists on the classic. With this variation, toasted coconut adds flavor and texture to the otherwise traditional filling. Hiding underneath all that gooey filling is a rich layer of chocolate ganache. This is one delicious, decadent, unforgettable dessert!

MAKES 8 TO 10 SERVINGS

FOR THE BASIC BUTTER PIE CRUST

1¼ cups (150 g) unbleached all-purpose flour

1 tsp (4 g) granulated sugar

½ tsp salt

½ cup (113 g) unsalted butter, cold, cut into small cubes

3 to 4 tbsp (45 to 60 ml) cold water

FOR THE FILLING

3 oz (85 g) **bittersweet chocolate**, roughly chopped

¼ cup (60 ml) **heavy cream**

1 cup (240 ml) **light corn syrup**

½ cup (100 g) granulated sugar

¼ cup (57 g) unsalted butter, melted and slightly cooled

3 large eggs

1 tsp (5 ml) vanilla extract

½ tsp salt

1¼ cups (150 g) **pecan halves**

1 cup (120 g) **sweetened shredded coconut**, toasted

TIP: To toast coconut, see page 167.

TO MAKE THE BASIC BUTTER PIE CRUST

Combine the flour, sugar and salt in a large bowl. Add the butter and mix with a pastry blender or a fork until the largest pieces of butter are about the size of large peas. Add the water, about a tablespoon (15 ml) at a time, and mix until a dough forms.

Shape the dough into a ball, place on a sheet of plastic wrap and flatten slightly into a disk about 1 inch (2.5 cm) thick. Wrap the dough tightly in plastic wrap and refrigerate for at least 2 hours.

Place the chilled pie dough on a lightly floured surface. Roll the dough into a circle ⅛ inch (0.3 cm) thick. Transfer the dough to a 9-inch (23-cm) pie pan. Trim and crimp the edges as desired. Place the pan in the refrigerator for about 30 minutes.

Preheat the oven to 325°F (160°C).

Line the chilled crust with a large piece of parchment paper, making sure to tuck the paper right up to the edges and sides of the crust. Fill the parchment paper with pie weights or uncooked beans so that they cover the bottom of the pan right up to the edges. Bake for 20 minutes. Remove the lining and weights. Bake the crust for 5 more minutes. Set aside.

TO MAKE THE FILLING

Increase the oven temperature to 350°F (180°C)

Place the chocolate in a heatproof bowl and set aside.

Place the cream in a small, heavy saucepan. Bring to a boil over medium heat. Pour the hot cream over the chocolate and let sit for 5 minutes. Then stir until smooth. Spread the chocolate mixture evenly in the bottom of the partially baked pie crust. Place the crust in the freezer while you make the remainder of the filling.

Stir together the corn syrup, sugar, butter, eggs, vanilla and salt until thoroughly combined. Stir in the pecans and coconut. Pour the mixture into the chilled crust. Place the pie on a parchment-lined baking sheet to catch any spills. Bake for 50 to 55 minutes, or until the crust is browned and the filling is set. Allow to cool for 20 minutes before serving.

OATMEAL CAKE WITH PEANUT BUTTER FROSTING

Oatmeal cakes have been around for ages. They're usually made with oats, nuts and coconut. While this one does indeed have oats and coconut, the nutty portion comes in the form of a crunchy peanut butter frosting. There's no shortage of flavor in this cake!

MAKES 16 SERVINGS

FOR THE CAKE

1 cup (80 g) **old-fashioned rolled oats**

1 cup (240 ml) boiling water

1½ cups (180 g) unbleached all-purpose flour

1 tsp (5 g) baking powder

1 tsp (5 g) baking soda

½ tsp ground cinnamon

½ tsp salt

½ cup (113 g) unsalted butter, softened

1 cup (200 g) firmly packed light brown sugar

½ cup (100 g) granulated sugar

2 large eggs

1½ tsp (7.5 ml) vanilla extract

½ cup (60 g) **sweetened shredded coconut**, toasted

FOR THE FROSTING

¼ cup (56 g) unsalted butter, softened

¼ cup (64 g) crunchy **peanut butter**

½ tsp vanilla extract

1½ cups (165 g) **confectioners' sugar**, sifted

2 tbsp (30 ml) **milk**

TO MAKE THE CAKE

Preheat the oven to 350°F (180°C). Grease an 8 x 8 x 2-inch (20 x 20 x 5-cm) baking pan.

Place the oats in a small bowl. Pour the boiling water over them, and set aside.

Whisk together the flour, baking powder, baking soda, cinnamon and salt. Set aside.

Using an electric mixer on medium speed, beat the butter, brown sugar and granulated sugar until light and fluffy. Add the eggs, one at a time, mixing well after each addition. Mix in the vanilla. Stir in the coconut and the oat mixture.

Reduce the mixer speed to low. Gradually add the flour mixture, and mix just until combined.

Transfer the batter to the prepared pan, and spread evenly. Bake for 40 to 45 minutes, or until a pick inserted into the center comes out clean. Set the pan on a wire rack to allow the cake to cool completely.

TO MAKE THE FROSTING

Using an electric mixer on medium speed, beat the butter, peanut butter and vanilla until thoroughly combined. Gradually add the confectioners' sugar, and mix well. Mix in the milk, beating until the frosting is smooth. Spread the frosting on top of the cooled cake.

TIP: For tips on toasting coconut, see page 167.

HAZELNUT CUPCAKES WITH CHOCOLATE-HAZELNUT FROSTING

The combination of chocolate and hazelnut is nothing short of fantastic. From my first bite of chocolate-hazelnut spread, I designated a permanent spot in my pantry for at least one jar. Here, that delicious spread stars in a sweet, creamy frosting that tops off simple cupcakes filled with toasted hazelnuts.

MAKES 24 CUPCAKES

FOR THE CUPCAKES

2½ cups (300 g) unbleached all-purpose flour

1½ tsp (7.5 g) baking powder

½ tsp baking soda

½ tsp salt

¾ cup (170 g) unsalted butter, softened

1½ cups (300 g) firmly packed light brown sugar

3 large eggs

2 tsp (10 ml) vanilla extract

1 cup (240 ml) **buttermilk**

1 cup (120 g) **hazelnuts**, toasted and chopped

FOR THE CHOCOLATE-HAZELNUT FROSTING

8 oz (227 g) **cream cheese**, softened

½ cup (113 g) unsalted butter, softened

½ cup (140 g) **chocolate-hazelnut spread**

2½ cups (275 g) **confectioners' sugar**, sifted

TO MAKE THE CUPCAKES

Preheat the oven to 350°F (180°C). Grease 24 standard muffin cups.

Whisk together the flour, baking powder, baking soda and salt. Set aside.

Using an electric mixer on medium speed, beat the butter and brown sugar until light and fluffy. Add the eggs, one at a time, mixing well after each addition. Mix in the vanilla.

Reduce the mixer speed to low. Add about a third of the flour mixture, and mix until a few streaks of flour remain. Mix in about half of the buttermilk. Add the remaining flour mixture in 2 portions, alternating with the remaining portion of buttermilk, mixing just until combined. Stir in the hazelnuts.

Divide the batter among the prepared muffin cups, filling each about half full. Bake for 18 to 22 minutes, or until a pick inserted into the center comes out clean. Allow to cool in the pans for 10 minutes. Then transfer the cupcakes to a wire rack to cool completely.

TO MAKE THE CHOCOLATE-HAZELNUT FROSTING

Using an electric mixer on medium speed, beat the cream cheese, butter and chocolate-hazelnut spread until blended and smooth. Gradually add the confectioners' sugar, and mix until smooth. Frost the cooled cupcakes.

TIP: To toast hazelnuts, place them in a single layer on a lined baking sheet. Bake at 350°F (180°C) for 10 to 15 minutes, or until browned and fragrant. If the hazelnuts have skins on them, place the toasted nuts on a kitchen towel and rub them with the towel to remove the skins easily.

COFFEE CARAMEL CHOCOLATE POKE CAKE

This beauty combines a simple chocolate cake with a caramel that's made with a coffee-flavored liqueur.
The caramel soaks into the cake, creating little pockets of rich caramel throughout the cake. Top it off
with chocolate whipped cream and a sprinkling of cocoa powder for an unforgettable dessert!

MAKES 24 SERVINGS

FOR THE CAKE

1¼ cups (150 g) unbleached all-purpose flour

1 tsp (5 g) baking powder

½ tsp baking soda

½ tsp salt

10 tbsp (141 g) unsalted butter, softened

1 cup (200 g) granulated sugar

¼ cup (50 g) firmly packed light brown sugar

2 large eggs

4 oz (113 g) **unsweetened chocolate**, melted and slightly cooled

½ tsp vanilla extract

½ cup (120 ml) **buttermilk**

FOR THE COFFEE CARAMEL

1 cup (200 g) granulated sugar

2 tbsp (30 ml) water

¼ cup (60 ml) **heavy cream**

2 tbsp (30 ml) **coffee-flavored liqueur**

Pinch of salt

FOR THE CHOCOLATE WHIPPED CREAM TOPPING

1 cup (240 ml) **heavy cream**

2 tbsp (25 g) granulated sugar

2 tsp (3 g) **unsweetened cocoa powder**, plus more for garnish

½ tsp vanilla extract

TO MAKE THE CAKE

Preheat the oven to 350°F (180°C). Grease a 9 x 13 x 2-inch (23 x 33 x 5-cm) baking pan.

Whisk together the flour, baking powder, baking soda and salt. Set aside.

Using an electric mixer on medium speed, beat the butter, granulated sugar and brown sugar until light and fluffy. Add the eggs, one at a time, mixing well after each addition. Mix in the cooled chocolate and vanilla. Reduce the mixer speed to low. Add about a third of the flour mixture, and mix until a few streaks of flour remain. Mix in about half of the buttermilk. Add the remaining flour mixture in 2 portions, alternating with the remaining portion of buttermilk, mixing just until combined.

Transfer the batter to the prepared pan and spread evenly. Bake for 35 to 40 minutes, or until a pick inserted into the center comes out clean. Allow the cake to cool in the pan for 10 minutes. Then poke ¼-inch (0.6-cm) holes about ¾ inch (2 cm) apart over the surface of the cake. I used the end of one of the beaters for my hand mixer.

TO MAKE THE COFFEE CARAMEL

Combine the granulated sugar and water in a heavy saucepan. Cook over medium heat until the sugar dissolves. Increase the heat to medium-high, and continue to cook until the mixture turns amber. Remove from the heat.

Add the cream (the mixture will bubble) and stir until combined. Stir in the liqueur and salt. Allow to cool and thicken for about 10 minutes. Pour the caramel evenly over the cake in the pan. Allow to cool to room temperature.

TO MAKE THE CHOCOLATE WHIPPED CREAM TOPPING

Place the cream in a large mixing bowl. Using an electric mixer with a whisk attachment, beat the cream at medium-high speed until it begins to thicken. Sprinkle the granulated sugar over the thickened cream and continue to mix until combined. Add the cocoa powder and vanilla, and continue to beat until you can lift the whisk out of the whipped cream and a peak that curves downward forms in the cream. Spread the whipped cream over the cooled cake. Sprinkle with cocoa powder.

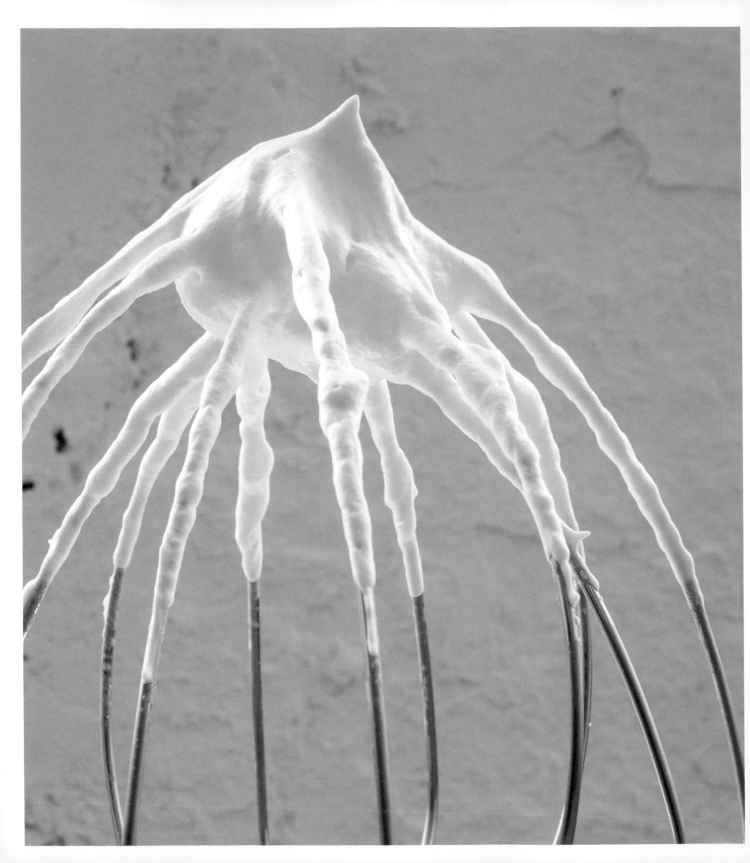

ACKNOWLEDGMENTS

Many thanks to Page Street Publishing for helping make this book a reality.

Much appreciation goes to Nan Lawrence, Tonya Kirk, Jane Hutchinson-Barefoot and Kerry Henry for their recipe testing help and encouragement. You ladies are lifesavers!

I must express my gratitude to the good people of Small Planet Digital for their taste-testing and feedback. It was so wonderful to know that the sheer volume of baked goods I made during the writing of this book didn't go to waste.

Most of all, thanks to Quinn for everything from helping with cleaning duty to listening to my random ideas to believing I could do this in the first place. You are absolutely the best.

ABOUT THE AUTHOR

Jennifer McHenry has been baking full-time since 2011 for bakeorbreak.com, the baking blog she started in 2006. But her baking tutelage began years before as a little girl alongside her grandmother in Mississippi. Her baking approach focuses on simple recipes that yield big results. Jennifer's work has been featured by *Southern Living*, MarthaStewart.com, *Huffington Post*, PBS and many others. She has been a longtime contributing blogger for the American Butter Institute and has developed recipes for numerous national brands. She now happily operates her mixer in Brooklyn, New York, alongside two hard-working cats and her husband, Quinn, who makes an affable sous baker.

INDEX